William Brodum

A Guide to Old Age

A Cure for the Indiscretions of Youth

William Brodum

A Guide to Old Age
A Cure for the Indiscretions of Youth

ISBN/EAN: 9783742816665

Manufactured in Europe, USA, Canada, Australia, Japa

Cover: Foto ©Andreas Hilbeck / pixelio.de

Manufactured and distributed by brebook publishing software (www.brebook.com)

William Brodum

A Guide to Old Age

A

GUIDE TO OLD AGE,

OR

A CURE

FOR THE

INDISCRETIONS

OF

YOUTH.

IN TWO VOLUMES.

BY WILLIAM BRODUM, M. D.

VIRGINIBUS PUERISQUE CANTO.———VIRGIL.
To Youths I write, and Virgins uninformed.

VOL. II.
THE FOURTH EDITION.

London:

Printed by J. W. MYERS, Paternoster-row,

FOR THE AUTHOR,

And sold at his House, No. 9, *Albion-street*, near the Leverian Museum, Blackfriar's-bridge, and may be had of all the Booksellers in the three Kingdoms.

1797.

[ENTERED AT STATIONERS-HALL.]

CONTENTS.

A.

*A*BERDEEN, *the diploma of its university to Doctor Brodum*   159
Action of the water in bathing   144
Addreſs from Dr. Brodum   153
Aetius on venery   19
A. R. his caſe, venereal   131
Aliments, of their nouriſhing qualities   23
Amazons, peculiarities incident to them   105
America, nervous cordial particularly efficacious there   186
Amorous pleaſures, evils occaſioned by them   21
Appearances, external ones highly neceſſary   167
Armitage General, dies in the act of coition   50
Aſia, females arrive at maturity, there ſooner than in Europe   85
Aſthma, a direction for it   173

B.

Bath, advice to those who bathe there	185
Bathing, in what recommended	115
Bilious Complaints, cure for it	171
Blindness occasioned through excessive venery	52
Boerhaave, on venereal cases	53
Botanical Syrup, its efficacy treated of	168, 169
directions for taking it	170
Boyle Mr. on the semen	47
Brodum Doctor, his address	153

C.

Caution to the public	162
Cleanliness necessary to health	141
Captain C. his Case, venereal	133
Coition, of persons who died in the act of it	50, 52, 56
brings on epileptic fits	54
Consumption occasioned by self-pollution	79
Cornelius Gallus, of his death in the act of coition	50
Corporeal powers, how affected by seminal liquor	24
Country, list of cures in various parts of it	188

D.

Deafness, those afflicted with it must personally attend	183
Didier Doctor, extraordinary case of epilepsy	54
Diploma granted to Doctor Brodum	159
Directions for taking the Nervous Cordial	170
Diseases of the head, a cure for them	172
natural to women, treated of	ibid.
Dropsy, a cure for it	174

E.

Epilepsy, remarkable cases of it	54
Eruptions in the face	168
Excessive venery, dreadful consequences of it	23
Exhalations of the skin treated of	67
External appearance to be regarded	167

F.

Female sex, their excesses in venery treated of	82
disorders incident to them treated of	97

G.

Gabius on the venereal disease	20
Galen on the venereal disease	28

H.

Haller on the venereal disease	29
Hippocrates, his remarks on the venereal disease	18
Hot-wells, Bristol, advice to those who bathe	185

I.

Infallible cure for a certain disorder	136

L.

Ladies in the decline of nature, how to act	173
Lettsom Doctor, his opinion on disorders incident to the female sex	100
Lord Chesterfield on cleanliness	141

M.

Mad, one made so by excessive venery	51
Matrix, a direction for the disorders of it	120
Memory impaired by self-pollution	60
Mind as well as the body affected by venery	63
Mole, a description of it	117
Morning best time for bathing	145

N.

Nerves, how affected in the heat of venery	61
Nervous disorders, how occasioned	71

*Nervous Cordial necessary for bathing in
    certain cases*   144

O.

Observations on sea-bathing   185
        the use of the Botanical Syrup   168
Onanism, extraordinary case of it   72
        observations on those addicted to it 174

P.

Palsy, a direction for it   174
*Parents, advice to them respecting their
    Children*   15
*Personal application, in what cases necessary
    to the doctor*   181
Personal consultation, when to be had   183
Places of sale for the doctor's medicines ibid.
Pleurisy, remarkable causes of it   56

R.

Regimen, general observations on it   175
*Remedy, an infallible one for a certain dis-
    order*   136
Rheumatism, a direction for it   174

S.

*Savage Monſ. gives an extraordinary vene-
    real case*   55

CONTENTS.

Sea bathing, observations on it	142
—— bathers, advice to them	185
Self-pollution, baneful effects of it	59
extraordinary cases of it	72
Semen, Galen's opinion of it	28
Sight, weakened by excessive venery	51
those afflicted with the loss of it to attend themselves	174
Social happiness, how promoted	169

T.

Tauvry, on the use of semen	35
Tunbridge Wells, in what cases bathing would be useful	115
Turbius, physician of Amsterdam, on the venereal disease	19

U.

University of Aberdeen, its diploma to Dr. Brodum	159
Urine, observations on it	26

V.

Van Swieton, on the venereal disease	55
Venereal excesses, observations thereon	13
Venereal cases, extraordinary ones	53, 54, 55, 56

CONTENTS.

Venus, extraordinary sacrifice to 53
Vespatius, on the venereal disease 20
Voice, altered by excessive venery 24
Voluptuaries, cold bath recommended to them 142

W.

Whites, a disorder so called, treated of 98
Women, at what age capable of bearing children 85

Y.

Young lady, extraordinary case of one 88, 89, 90
Youth, one destroys his constitution by self-pollution. 75
　　one dies in consequence of self-pollution 80
　　how to take the Botanical Syrup 170

A GUIDE TO OLD AGE.

CHAP. XX.

Of Weaknesses contracted before Marriage, with proper Advice in every Respect whatever.

VENEREAL EXCESSES.

EXTREMES, says an old adage, are dangerous: and there is nothing more true in politics, in philosophy, or in medicine; than this motto. A volume might be written with the utmost ease, deduced from the nature of things, and from the actual history of mankind at large, to prove the multitude of evils both

both of body and mind, that encounter a ſtate of perpetual celibacy and abſtraction from ſexual delights. But as I write not profeſſedly on this ſubject at preſent, I ſhall leave the deſcription of theſe evils and inconveniencies to thoſe who are beſt acquainted with the humours and caprices of the mind, the defects and debilities of the corporeal functions, which are daily witneſſed in convents of the ſeverer orders of nuns and friars in Roman Catholic countries, and in the domeſtic circles of bachelors and old maids, in countries where ſuch orders are prohibited; and ſhall paſs on to the conſideration of thoſe evils and calamities which naturally accrue from a conduct diametrically the reverſe; the exceſſive, and more eſpecially the too early, indulgence in venereal purſuits and gratifications.

And

And here, let no man think me an enemy to the rational pleasures, the intermingled blifs of fexual delights; fuch as, for the wifeft purpofes, the Almighty Parent has created our bodies, mutually to give and receive, and has deftined us univerfally to poffefs.

" Be ye fruitful and multiply," was the original and divine command; and it is that this command may be duly executed that I now write. Not to extenuate but to enlarge the circle of felicity; not to diminifh but to increafe the numbers of mankind.

To you, ye parents, therefore, I addrefs myfelf, whofe maturer years, and more confummate knowledge, muft make you better acquainted with the importance of this delicate fubject, fhould you even have efcaped thofe fatal rocks on which fo many thoufands have fplit, split, and preserved your constitutions pure and inviolate, to the infinite benefit and advantage of your children, undepraved by disease, uninjured by youthful contagion, to you I address myself, and request that, if you retain any value for the health you possess, any regard for the future prosperity of the family entrusted to your care, you will instruct them early in the precepts this little volume is designed to inculcate, and the evils it attempts to point out. But chiefly to you do I direct my attention, ye candid and ingenuous youths, who, just freed from the shackles of a professional or a college education, are cast at large on the world's wide stage, in the thoughtless giddiness of youth, devoid of maturer judgment, and without any friendly mentor to guide aright your heedless footsteps. Attend to the advice which a friend to your unsuspecting age thus publicly offers; hear his

report

report on the dangers which furround you; receive with veneration his addrefs; and practife his falutary precepts. So fhall you pafs filently on to the winter of unimbittered age, indulge in every rational gratification you were created to partake of, and enjoy yourfelves to the lateft hour of life, free from thofe difeafes whofe evil effects he who addreffes himfelf to you, has moft particularly ftudied, and moft amply witneffed, and which, in moft inftances, require the utmoft fagacity of the phyfician, even to palliate and foften.

The greateft phyficians of antiquity, who have tranfmitted their names to us with the higheft renown, and who will be read and admired whilft letters and fcience retain their influence, have defcribed the evils that are occafioned by the abufe of amorous pleafures, under the title *Tabes Dorfalis*. Hippocrates fays,

says, that this diforder arifes from fome defect in the fpinal marrow. Young married people, who have formerly indulged in illicit amours, and thofe of a lafcivious difpofition, are particularly afflicted with it. They have no fever, and, though they eat well, they fall away and become confumptive. They feel as if a fting or ftitch defcended from the head, along the fpinal marrow. Every time they go to ftool, or have occafion to urine, they fhed a great quantity of feminal liquor. They are incapable of procreation, though they frequently dream of the act of coition. Walking, particularly in rugged paths, puts them out of breath, and weakens them; occafioning a heavinefs in the head, and noife in the ears, which are fucceeded by a general marafmus, and fometimes a violent fever, which terminates their days. Such are the words of Hippocrates, which correfpond with
what

what Aetius says upon the same subject. Young people have the air and appearance of old age. They become frail, effeminate, benumbed, lazy, stupid, and incapable of any action. Their bodies are bent from debility, and their legs are swelled from the same cause, and unable to perform their usual functions; they have an utter distaste for the festive scenes of life, and for every thing of business are totally incapacitated; many also, observes this accurate historian, become paralytic.

The stomach is disordered; all the whole frame is weakened; paleness, universal decay, and emaciation succeed.

These opinions are supported by Turbius, that celebrated physician of Amsterdam; these are the words which occur in his treatise on this subject:
" The

" The spinal marrow does not only waste, but the body and mind both equally languish, and the man perishes a miserable victim."

" Samuel Vesputius," continues he, " was seized with a flux of humours, extremely acrid, which immediately affected the hind part of the head, and the nape of the neck, from whence it communicated to the spinal marrow, the loins, the buttocks, and the articulation of the thighs, which made this unfortunate man suffer such excruciating pain, that his countenance was entirely distorted, and he was seized with a slow fever, which, by degrees, consumed him; but not so fast as he desired; and he was in such a situation, that he frequently invoked death before he was snatched from his misery." To these opinions, we shall add that of the celebrated Gaubius, in
his

his Pathological and Medicinal Inftitutes: " An early emiffion of feed is not only prejudicial, by reafon of the lofs of a moft ufeful humour, but likewife by a repetition of the convulfive motion by which it is difcharged; for the higheft pleafure is followed by an univerfal refolution of the natural powers, which cannot frequently take place without deftroying all the ftamina of the conftitution. Befides, the more the ftrainers of the body are drained, the more humour they draw to them from the other parts, and the juices being thus conveyed to the genitals, the other parts are impoverifhed. Hence it is, that from exceffive venery, arife laffitude, weaknefs, numbnefs, a feeble gait, head-achs, convulfions of the fenfes, but efpecially of the fight, and dulnefs of hearing, an ideot look, a feverifh circulation of blood, exficcation, leannefs, a confumption of the lungs.

lungs and back, and want of all mafculine powers. Thefe evils are increafed, and become incurable by reafon of a perpetual itch for pleafure, which neverthelefs the inclinations of the mind, as well as the paffions of the body, ftill defire ardently; from whence it follows, as before obferved, that they have obfcene dreams in fleep, and the prone parts, upon every flight occafion, have an ineffectual tendency to ftiffen, and the quantity of replaced femen will be difcharged from the relaxed cells (however fmall, it becomes a burthen and a ftimulus) by the flighteft efforts. Thus it is, that thefe exceffes bring fuch perdition upon the flower of our youth."

Such then are the fentiments of thefe great men, at different periods, upon the confequence of too violent feminal emiffions; and, to illuftrate what has been premifed, premised, it will be necessary to pay some attention to the importance of this liquor, with respect to the well-being of the whole human machine.

It may, with truth, be said, that our bodies are in a continual state of decay; to repair this waste, nature has furnished us with nutrition, by assistance of aliments, at due times introduced into the stomach; but whenever this supply of food is wanting, or is converted to any partial purpose, and not to the general nutrition of the body at large, our frame must necessarily decay much faster, and more quickly sink into a state of extreme debility, and total weakness. Too copious evacuations are the most frequent causes of this debility; for our bodies are so constructed, that for the aliments to acquire the degree of preparation necessary for the reparation of general strength, a certain quantity

quantity of humours muſt be previouſly ſecreted, and conſtantly at hand. If this condition is wanting, if the debilitated ſtomach is incapable of performing its office, the digeſtion and concoction of the aliments are imperfect in proportion, as the deficient humour happens to be of a more elaborate kind, or of greater importance to animal œconomy.

The ſeminal liquor has ſo great an influence upon the corporeal powers, and upon perfect digeſtion, which repairs them, that phyſicians of all ages have been unanimouſly of opinion, that the loſs of an ounce of this humour would weaken more than that of forty ounces of blood. An idea may be formed of its importance, by obſerving the effects it produces as ſoon as it begins to be formed; the voice, the phyſiognomy, the features of the face change, the beard grows, and the body often

often takes another appearance, becauſe the muſcles acquire a thickneſs and firmneſs, which form a ſenſible difference between the body of an adult perſon, and that of a youth not yet arrived at the age of puberty.

Theſe changes are prevented by deſtroying the organ which ſerves to ſecrete the liquor that produces it; and Boerhaave obſerved, that the amputation of the teſticles, at the age of virility, made the beard fall, and effeminated the voice.

There are humours, ſuch as perſpiration, which quit the body the moment they are ſeparated from the circulating veſſels.

There are others, ſuch as urine, which after this ſeparation, are retained for a certain time in the reſervoirs destined for that purpose; and from whence they do not issue till they are collected in a sufficient quantity, to excite an irritation upon these reservoirs, which mechanically cause them to empty themselves. There is a third sort, which are secreted and retained in the manner of the second, in reservoirs, not with the design of being completely evacuated, but to acquire on these reservoirs a degree of perfection which qualifies them for fresh functions, when they return into the mass of humours. Such, amongst others, is the genital liquor. Being separated in the testicles, this liquor passes from hence in a pretty long canal into the veficulæ seminales, is continually reforbed by the vessels adapted for that purpose, and is gradually restored to the mass of humours. Many evidences might be produced to demonstrate this fact; amongst others, for instance, the secretion of the seminal

nal liquor in a healthy man, is conſtantly made in the teſticles; it repairs to the reſervoirs, the limits of which are very confined, and cannot, perhaps, contain all that is ſecreted in a day. There are, neverthelefs, ſome reſerved and continent men, who have no evacuations of this kind for many months; in theſe, it muſt, therefore, return into the veſſels of circulation, which is greatly facilitated by the ſtructure of the organs which aſſiſts in the ſecretion of this humour, in conveying it into the proper channel, and in preſerving it. The veins are there much more confiderable than the arteries, and in a proportion not to be found elſewhere. And ſuppofing, according to modern opinions*, that no other than the lymphatic veins abſorb, the genital parts are equally

* Vide, Dr. Monro, jun. De Vaſis Lymphaticis; Dr. Hunter, the Medical Commentaries, &c.

suited to a considerable absorption, as the vessels of this kind are there very numerous.

Though Galen was unacquainted with the mechanism of the semen, he, was not ignorant that the humours were enriched by their being retained; for, as he says, every part is full of this liquor, in those who refrain from any commerce with women; but those who frequently give way to this intercourse, are quite deficient in this humour. He then enters into a curious disquisition, in order to ascertain how small a quantity of this liquor can communicate infinite strength to the body, and concludes, that it has excellent virtue, and may, therefore, very speedily convey some of its power to all parts of the corporeal machine; and that as small causes often produce great effects, he

thinks

thinks it is no way surprising, that the testicles should furnish liquor proper to circulate fresh vigour over all the body, as the brain produces many motions and sensations, and the heart communicates the power of beating to the arteries. To this may be properly added what that great professor Haller says upon the same subject. His words are, " The semen is kept in the vesiculæ seminales until the man makes use of it. During this period, the quantity that is then confined excites him to acts of venery; but the great part of this seed, which is the most volatile and odoriferous, as well as the strongest, is absorbed into the blood, and then produces upon its return very surprising changes; it makes the beard, hair, and nails grow; it changes the voice and manners; for age does not produce those changes in animals; it is the semen only that performs these operations,

tions, as we find eunuchs are not fufceptible of them."

This liquor is a ftimulus or provocative, which irritates the parts it touches, as its powerful feat, and the manifeft irritation it communicates to the organs of generation, plainly evince.

Thefe fharp particles being thus inceffantly abforbed and re-united with the humour, they create a gentle, though conftant ftimulus in the veffels, which thereby more forcibly contract and more eafily act upon the fluids; hence circulation is quickened; nutrition performed with greater regularity, and every other animal function becomes more perfect.

This being the cafe, eunuchs muft neceffarily be, in many refpects, deficient in their animal œconomy; but if
they

they are incapable of the advantages that are derived from the abforption of this liquor, they are, on the other hand, not deprived of that precious part of the blood which is allotted for *femen*, and, of courfe, they are not liable to thofe changes which are occafioned by the prepared feminal liquor; nor are they expofed to thofe diforders which arife from the privation of this humour unprepared. When the firft is not feparated, the animal machine will be deficient in thofe fuccours which it derives from the prepared femen, without being liable to the alterations which depend thereupon,; but this can in no refpect weaken; if, on the one hand, it gains nothing, fo, on the other, it lofes nothing; the body of an eunuch may, therefore, in this refpect, be confidered in a ftate of childhood.

To what has been here faid upon this fubject, the obfervations of the celebrated

brated profeffor Skmeider, of Leipfic; will be no improper fupplement.

Whilft I have been fometimes meditating on various natural fubjects, fays this profeffor, fuch as the human body, the ftructure of it, its motion, its humours, &c. I imagined that amongft other things, the genital liquor well deferved to be carefully examined; and, by enquiring into the nature, the conftituent parts, the veffels, receptacles, and fecretion of it, I have recollected fome things concerning its motion; not that which is ejaculatory and excited in coition, or by another filthy titillation; nor its own private and inteftine motion, which, that it muft have, we are pretty fure of, from the fpirituous and fulphurous particles it abounds with; but the motion I mean, is a progreffive one, from its receptacles back again into the mafs of the blood; and

and several circumstances have induced me to believe and assert, that there really is such a motion, till such time as the contrary shall be plainly and evidently demonstrated to me. To get some light in this matter, I perused various authors, both ancient and modern, philological as well as anatomical, but to little or no purpose, for I have been scarce able to find any thing in them concerning this progressive or circulatory motion, except in Hippocrates, in his book *De Genitura*, from whose words we may conclude he was of this opinion, as he says, " As soon as there is seed made, the flesh and outward skin become more porous, and the little veins are more opened than they were before; but those who are yet in their childhood, or else eunuchs, have, for that reason, no hair either on the pubes or chin, and are all over smooth, because no passage being yet made

made for the feed, the outward superfices are no where rarified, for the paffage to the feed, as I have faid a little before, is ftopped up."

From thefe words it is evident, that Hippocrates has made mention of this progrefs of the feed into the body; whilft he afferts, that by this fame feed the flefh and outward fkin are rarefied, that the beard and hair on the pubes might come through, becaufe there is a paffage made for the feed, which, before the years of puberty, and in eunuchs, is yet ftopped up. Rolfinch juft hints at it, and at the fame time denies the circulation of the feed, as will appear from his words:. " The oftentatious name of circulation, gives no reft to the curious; the femen feems neither to circulate within nor without the tefticles; the vigour which the tefticles add to the body ought not to be afcribed to their bulk, but to their power;

power; yet I will not deny, that some seminal atoms may be mixed with the blood, from the remainder of what serves for the nutrition of the testicles, and which is received back into the veins." That these words intimate a regress of the seed into the blood, is undeniable; but they are not strong enough, and a few atoms are not sufficient to procure the body that strength and vigour which, cæteris paribus, it will ever possess, and which no small or accidental intermixture can produce. Tauvry, speaking of the use of the seed, in regard to the body it is made in, and considering it on account of the visible effects it derives upon the body, comes without doubt, into the opinion of its circulatory motion. I shall transcribe the passage entire; it is worth reading, and runs thus:
" Nobody doubts, but that we owe our origin to the seed, and that whilst it generates in us other beings very like ourselves,

felves, it renders us as it were immortal. But it is more difficult to trace and know the ufe it is of to the fubject in which it is produced; yet we fee it gives us a certain degree of perfection, ftrength, and vigour; becaufe eunuchs, women, and thofe who, by exceffive venery, are enervated, become like children, daftardly and imperfect. For the fame reafon it produces a beard, and renders the voice of a deeper found; and as between eunuch and woman, there is no difference, in what relates to the production of this liquid, it is very probable, that this liquid returning into the mafs of the blood, is the caufe of thefe remarkable effects."

Thefe are the arguments of our author, to which I fhall add my own reafons, to confirm this opinion.

The firft and moft cogent is the fmallnefs of the feminal bags, and the continual

nual and daily afflux into them. That they are small, we are convinced by our own eyes; for they are not three inches in length, and hardly one inch in breadth and thickness; though on one side they are commonly somewhat bigger than they are on the other. Now, let any one well consider the smallness of these vessels, and the daily influx of seed into them, which nobody can deny, unless he denies likewise, against all reason and experience, the circulation of the blood, the undoubted cause of secretion of all humours in the body, whether good or bad: Now let any one consider well the smallness of the seminal bags, that are no ways capable of receiving and containing such a quantity of seed as may be made in seven or eight weeks, (I will not say in several years) and so long till a man cohabits with a woman. As these things are then incompatible, it is necessary that the semen should be carried off

off again to the mafs of the blood or the body, for the reafons already alledged by Tauvry, and others that may be given.

Secondly, the change that is obferved in the temperament of the body after caftration, is a corroborating evidence of the progreffive motion of the femen; for it is manifeft, that animals when their tefticles are taken away, grow fatter, are more languid, and lefs courageous. This in all ages has been a fact fo notorious, that there is not a gregarious male animal maintained, to fatisfy the wants or the luxuries of man, but has been obliged from time immemorial to fubmit to the favage practife of caftration, that his food may be eaten with greater reft, unlefs indeed he be fimply preferved for the purpofes of propagation. It is likewife, amongft other things, to be obferved, that in eunuchs the hair of the beard and privities does

not

not fall off before caſtration; and that if it is not on the chin, at the time of the operation, and other parts, it never will appear in the ſame manner as it does upon thoſe who have not undergone it. The privation of virility likewiſe changes the voice, which becomes more ſharp after ſuch privation. It is reported of ſtags that are fit for copulation, that if immediately after ſhedding their horns, which fall off every year, they are deprived of the powers of procreation, no new horns will grow in future.

Who reports this and when? Let the author's name be mentioned; are not theſe two laſt diſeaſes the ſame? This motion and exiſtence in the blood of the ſeed is moreover proved from the rank ſmell of ſome beaſts, and the taſte in the fleſh of others, as, alſo from the ſtated period on which their deſire of copula-

copulation returns. What becomes of all this feed? Where is it hid when thofe animals do not couple with their females? Therefore to fay that no fecretion of femen is made, is fpeaking againft all reafon and experience. Organs are fet apart for that fecretion, which according to the laws of nature, are conftantly employed in their office. And there is a perpetual fupply of matter, or arterial blood, from which the feed is feparated. We are likewife taught by experience, the prefence of feed in male and adult animals who have never been caftrated, at all times. Whenever an animal is diffected, the feed bags will appear turgid with recent feed. . I am, moreover, of opinion, that if the femen did not circulate in the body, it would be utterly impoffible for unmarried men to abftain from fornication, by reafon of the continual increafe of feed, and the inceffant irritations it would

would otherwife occafion to abominable luft; not to mention the various and moft dangerous diforders it would produce by its fuperabundance, if it could not be any way diminifhed, except by copulation. It is true, that a man may difturb and injure the motion of the feed, by exceffes in diet, and various meats, and liquors, that either augment the quantity of femen too much, render it fharp, or elfe obftruct the veffels, and fo caufe a corruption and ftagnation of the feed, and an acrimony contracted from thence, ought fometimes to be reckoned amongft the morbific caufes of a *furor uterinus, priapifm, and fatyriafis.* This is evident from what has often been obferved in women troubled with the *furor uterinus;* namely, that upon rubbing the pudenda with mufk, or ambergrife, or giving them clyfters of the fame kind, great quantities of fperm liquid are difcharged, with imme-

immediate relief to the patient. From what has been said, I think it is manifest, that the seed, from its vessels, returns into the blood, after its secretion, and from the blood is again secreted into the spermatic vessels.

The whole of the interior as well as the exterior part of the body, is covered with absorbent vessels: hence the chyle is absorbed from the stomach and intestines, and passes into the thoracic duct, and from thence again into the general circulation of the blood: hence, in dropsical complaints, the moisture of the air is by the same process continually entering the pores of the skin, and enlarging the cavity of the abdomen, or the cellular membrane universally spread over the body; and hence, in many large abscesses, where the pus is deep, and the quantity considerable, we frequently see the tumour suddenly dispersed, and another

another tumour immediately formed in fome neighbouring fituation; or the pus forming the tumour, may perhaps pafs off, in confequence of the action of the fame abforbent or lymphatic fyftem, by the inteftines, the urinary veffels, or even the veffels fecreting the faliva into the mouth: this operation of nature is termed by phyficians *tranflation* or *metaftafis*. It is the fame procefs, and the action of the fame fyftem of veffels, diftributed around the proftate gland, the vafa deferentia, and the tunica albuginea of the teftes, that produces the reabforption of the feminal liquor into the blood veffels, and ferves as an effectual anfwer to the queftion which has fo often been propofed by phyfiologifts, " where are the paffages through which the femen returns to the blood?"

But though in this manner we are acquainted with the caufe of action in

fuch

such tranflations and changes of pofition, we know not the exprefs laws by which it is guided, or the reafons why, in any change or tranflation it fhould prefer one fituation or pofition to another; we cannot predict on the fudden difperfion of a tumor, whether it will be a morbid or a falutary difperfion; or whether the matter contained therein, when thus re-abſorbed, will pafs away by urine or by the inteſtines; or whether it will again fix itfelf in fome other fituation, as on the lungs; for example, or in any other part of the body. We cannot tell why the venereal virus, after abſorption has once taken place, fhould affect the glands of the tonfils, rather than thofe of the axilla, or the parotid glands; nor why an abforption of cantharides into the fyftem fhould affect the urinary bladder in particular, and produce ftranguary.--- There are myfteries in medicine, as well as in philofophy; and it is more laudable

to

to avow our ignorance openly, than to screen it under long words of no meaning, or hypotheses of no foundation in nature. It is impossible, by any general laws which have yet been discovered, to account for the phenomena above taken notice of; and still more impossible is it to account for the passage which many hard substances take after having been swallowed, such as pins, needles, and other pointed spicula, and which have at length been brought away through the urinary or other passages, with the urine or other fluids, discharging themselves externally, of which we have had many examples attested by authors of credit and veracity. Vide Miscell. &c.

Which way could these things get into the urinary or other vessels? That the blood carried them with it, through the arteries, veins, and capillary vessels, is very difficult to conceive. Let any one who

who underſtands anatomy weigh and conſider the curious progreſs, and many crooked windings, even the chyle is forced to make in its paſſage from the ſtomach to the ſubclavian vein. Let him conſider the various windings and capillary veſſels through which the blood circulates, and compare it with the courſe of theſe hard ſubſtances, and then judge with what difficulty they muſt be carried to the ſecretary organs of the urine, and with the ſame facility be ſeparated from the blood, as the urine is, without wounding the veſſels through which they paſs. The above-mentioned Tauvry is of opinion, that the ſeed through the pores of the veins goes back into the maſs of blood, which regreſs he conceives to be made in this manner: The ſeed, ſays he, included in its veſſel, ferments, and, by continuing there, acquires a conſtitution it was not before endowed with; that is, it gains ſome-

thing

thing by increafe of motion, and is more fubtilized; fo that returning into the mafs of blood, it there brings forth thofe alterations, which it could not have produced, unlefs it had been rectified and exalted in the feminal veffels.

When thefe veffels are once filled, and more feminal matter comes to that which is contained in them, it is thus forced by degrees to pafs off into the pores of the veins, and circulating with the blood, by its glutinous quality, in a manner, involves and withholds its more fpirituous particles, and hinders the diffipation of them. This is a great reafon that in the act of coition great quantities of this oily fubftance are, by repetition, exhaufted, and the fpirits evaporated; and from this principle arifes the debility of thofe who are deftitute of this liquor. Mr. Boyle is of the fame opinion. As to myfelf, I believe that
the

the feed being attenuated and fubtilized in the tefticles and feminal veffels, returns by the lymphatic veffels, which afcends towards the abdomen, and then they difcharge their lymph into the fanguiferous veffels; and that after this manner it is carried again into the circulation, to the great benefit of the whole body. I heartily wifh, that the moft fkilful anatomift, and phyfiological writers of the greateft penetration, would make further enquiry into this affair, the certain knowledge of which would be of great utility.

From thefe obfervations, I think it is clearly proved, that the fuperabundant femen is abforbed by the lymphatic veffels into the body, where it communicates frefh circulation and vigour, and difperfes ftrength and power to every part of it.

If

If then this liquor is of such eminent importance to the proper functions of the whole machine, let us consider what may be the effects of too great and improper a discharge of it.

Ætius has handed down to us a description of the ills that are produced by too great an emission of the semen: " Young people of this description, says he, have the air and appearance of old age; they become pale, effeminate, benumbed, lazy, base, stupid, and imbecile; their bodies are bent, their legs not able to carry them; they have an utter distaste for every thing, are totally incapacitated, and many times become paralytic;" and he therefore includes amorous pleasures among the number of the six causes which occasion the palsy. Galen observes, that the same causes occasion disorders of the brain and nerves, and destroy the muscular powers;

he tells us, that a patient under his care, for a violent diforder not being perfectly recovered, died the fame night that he paid the conjugal tribute to his wife. And Pliny, the naturalift, informs us, that Cornelius Gallus, the ancient prætor, and Titus Etherius, the Roman knight, died in the very act of coition. Gen. Armitage is another proof of the truth of the affertion. Sanctorius, who has examined with the greateft attention all the caufes which actuate our bodies, has obferved, after Ætius, that this weakens the ftomach, deftroys digeftion, obftructs the infenfible perfpiration, an irregularity in the difcharge of which produces the moft fatal confequences, occafions the liver and reins to be overheated, gives a difpofition for the ftone in the kidnies, and ufually occafions the lofs of, or at leaft weakens the fight. Lommius, in his Commentaries upon Celfus, obferves, that too frequent emiffions sions of the seed relax, dry up, weaken, enervate, and produce a crowd of evils, such as apoplexies, lethargies, epilepsies, faintings, the loss of sight, tremors, palsy, spasm, and every species of the most racking gout. Schelaumer says, that too great a dissipation of the animal spirits weakens the stomach, destroys the appetite, and nutrition no longer taking place, the motion of the heart is weakened, all the parts languish, and an epilepsy succeeds. Salmuth has seen a learned man of a splenetic constitution go mad; and another man, whose brain was so dried up, that it was heard to rattle in the pericranium; and both these disorders were occasioned by excesses of the same nature. And the author of Memoirs of Curious Naturalists (De Cun 2. Ann. 5. Append. Obs. 88. p. 56.) says, that he has seen a man 59 years of age, who, three weeks after marriage with a young woman, fell suddenly

denly blind, and died at the end of four months, which he attributed to the exceſſive libidinous diſpoſition of the wife, and the too frequent gratification of the huſband. The celebrated Hoffman tells us (in his book De Morbis et Eximia Venere) that a young man of 18 years of age, who had frequent connections with a ſervant girl, was on a ſudden ſeized with a weakneſs, and a general tremor in all his limbs, his face became red, and his pulſe very weak. He was relieved from this ſtate in an hour's time; but an inceſſant languor continued on him. The ſame fit frequently returned, and threw him into great agonies, which, at the end of eight days, occaſioned a contraction and tumor in the right arm, with a pain in his right elbow, which was greatly increaſed in its ſize.

The

The diforder continued augmenting for a confiderable time, notwithftanding many remedies were prefcribed. At length, however, the doctors performed a cure upon this patient. Boerhaave fays, that the lofs of too much femen occafions laffitude, debilitates, and renders exercife difficult, it caufes convulfions, emaciation, and pains in the membrane of the brain; it deadens the fenfes, and particularly the fight; it gives rife to a dorfal confumption, and various other diforders, which are connected with thefe. He alfo fays, that he had feen a patient, whofe diforder began by laffitude, and a weaknefs in all parts of the body, particularly towards the loins; it was attended with an involuntary motion of the tendons, periodical fpafms, and bodily decay, infomuch, as to deftroy the whole corporeal frame; he felt a pain even in the membrane of the brain, a pain which patients call

call a dry burning heat, and which inceſſantly affected the moſt noble parts. He ſays, that he has likewiſe ſeen a young man afflicted with a dorſal conſumption, who, though he was frequently cautioned not to give way to amorous pleaſures, neverthelefs ſo far yielded to their impulſe, that his body, before his death, was quite deformed, and the fleſhy ſubſtance which appears above the ſpinal apophyſes of the loins, was entirely waſted; and that even the brain was in ſome meaſure conſumed.

Coition brings on epileptic fits, in thoſe who are ſubject to them; and, to this cauſe Van Swieten attributes the great oppreſſion the patients ſuffer if the fits are frequent.

Dr. Didier knew a merchant of Montpellier, who never made any ſacrifices to Venus without having a fit of epilepſy.
Galen

Galen furnishes us with a similar instance, as well as Henry Van Steers. Van Swieten knew a man, who was troubled with the epilepsy, who had a fit upon his wedding-night.

Hoffman was acquainted with a very lascivious woman, who usually had a fit of epilepsy after each act of venery. Boerhaave observes, that in the heat of venery, all the nerves are affected, oftentimes even fatally; and gives an example of a woman, who, every time she performed an act of coition, fell into a pretty long sincope; and another of a man, who died the very first time he copulated with a woman, the spasm being so violent, that it brought on a general palsy.

Monsieur Savage has given us a very extraordinary instance of a man, who was

was seized with a spasm in the very middle of enjoyment, whereby his whole body became stiff, he lost all sensation and memory, and the fit continued upon him for twelve years.

Thus we find that excessive indulgence in amorous pleasure does not only produce languishing disorders, but frequently those of an acute and violent nature, and it constantly impedes the cure of complaints derived from another source. Hoffman, after speaking of the dangerous effects of amorous pleasure for those who labour under wounds, considers those risks which persons run, 'by addicting themselves to it, who are frequently afflicted with fevers. Upon this occasion, he quotes an observation of Fabricius de Hilden, who says, that a man having copulated with a woman the tenth day after a pleurisy, which had terminated

on

on the seventh, by abundant perspiration, was seized with a violent fever, and immediate trembling, and died on the thirteenth day. He also relates, that a man of a gouty disposition, much addicted to women and wine, who fancying himself cured of a pleurisy, was, immediately after coition, seized with a violent trembling all over his body, extreme flushing in the face, attended by all the symptoms of the disorder, which he thought had been expelled, but which returned with much greater violence than at first, and he was in far greater danger. He also mentions a man, who never yielded to venereal excesses, without having an intermitting fever for several days.

If such then are the fatal accidents produced by the excessive indulgence of amorous passions in a natural and legitimate

timate way, how much more baneful muſt be the effects which flow from the gratification of them in an unnatural and illegitimate manner, which I ſhall illuſtrate in the ſucceeding chapters.

CHAP.

CHAP. XXI.

Dissertation on the baneful Effects of Self-pollution in the Male Sex.

WE have already seen the concurrent testimonies of the most eminent physicians, with regard to the fatal consequences of excessive indulgence in amorous pleasure in a natural way; the subject of this section is the consideration of the still more direful effects of seminal discharges in an unnatural channel; for, as a celebrated philologist observes, " The loss of too great a quantity of semen in the natural manner, is attended by very dangerous consequences; but they are still more dreadful, when the same quantity

quantity has been diffipated in an unnatural manner; for the evils which happen to thofe who wafte themfelves in a natural way, are very alarming, but thofe which are occafioned by felf-pollution are ftill more fhocking."

It would, indeed, be of very infignificant confequence, in a phyfical fenfe, whether this evacuation was occafioned by either of the methods I have ftated, if they are alike pernicious, but the manner is, in this refpect, equal to the fubftance. Sanctorius points out to us the caufe of the peculiar evils arifing from felf-pollution. He fays, " mode-
" rate coition is ufeful, when nature
" folicits for it; when it is folicited by
" the imagination, it weakens all the
" faculties, particularly the memory."
This may be very clearly exemplified; when we are in a ftate of health, we have no amorous defires, but when

the

the *veſiculæ ſeminalis* are replete with a quantity of liquor, which has acquired ſuch a degree of thickneſs, as to render its return into the maſs of blood difficult; and, in theſe circumſtances, when an evacuation takes place, we may be partly certain, that the corporeal frame will not thereby ſuffer any ſenſible diminution of ſtrength. But ſuch the ſtructure of the genital organs, that they are actuated, and the ſucceeding deſires are animated, not only by the preſence of the ſuperabundant ſeminal humour, but alſo by the imagination, which having great influence upon theſe parts, may, by being occupied with laſcivious deſires, give them ſuch a diſpoſition, as to create theſe deſires, the gratification whereof is the more pernicious, in proportion as it is unneceſſary to the welfare of the body. Theſe organs, like the others, are never properly actuated, but when nature ſtimulates

mulates them; for example, the want of food and drink, is indicated by hunger and thirſt; and exceſſes, in either reſpect, are prejudicial by enfeebling the body. The neceſſity of going to ſtool, and voiding urine, is ſignified by certain phyſical conditions, but a bad habit may ſo far pervert the conſtitution of the organs, that the neceſſity of theſe evacuations may no longer depend upon the quantity of matter to be evacuated. We ſubject ourſelves to want, when not neceſſitated; and this is preciſely the caſe of thoſe who addict themſelves to ſelf-pollution. Imagination and cuſtom, not nature and reaſon, prompt them to this filthy practice. Nature is drained of one of her moſt eſſential humours, and which ſhe ſo viſibly points out the application of for her own ſupport, and the perpetuation of the human ſpecies. Habit will, neverthelefs, in time

time so far pervert nature, that, in confequence of that law of the animal œconomy, whereby humours are attracted by irritation, there will be a continual conflux of humours upon thefe parts; for, as Hippocrates obferves, when a man habituates himfelf to feminal emiffions, the veffels that are therein employed, are unneceffarily dilated, and the femen is, by that means, more abundantly attracted. Not only the body, but the mind, is contaminated, for no fooner has this uncleannefs fixed its empire in the heart, but from that time it purfues the man continually, and never relinquifhes its dominion.

Even upon the moft ferious and awful occafions, he will find himfelf tranfported with luftful conceptions and defires, which inceffantly purfue him, and occupy his imagination. The self-polluter, entirely devoted to this practice, is liable, on that account, to the same diforders, as the metaphysician, or the mathematician, whose attention is engrossed by a single object; and it is universally allowed, that nothing debilitates the faculties more than the mind being constantly engaged upon the same subject; for that part of the brain which is then occupied makes an effort, similar to that of a muscle, which has been for a long time considerably extended; this occasions such a continual motion in the part as cannot be stopped, or such fixed attention, that the idea cannot be changed. Self-polluters are under the same predicament, or else they are completely incapacitated; so that when their faculties are not entirely destroyed, they are afflicted with all the diforders incident to the brain, the hypochondria, epilepsy, catalepsy,

lepsy, insensibility, imbecility, nervous disorders, &c. &c.

Disorders, when thus produced, are an additional incentive to their cause; as the patient flatters himself with momentary relief, from the gratification of a disposition that perpetually engages his attention; and therefore, he daily and hourly encreases his misery, and saps the very essence of existence.

If to this we add the difficulty that frequently attends the indulgence of amorous passions in a natural way, the expence naturally attendant, the risk with regard to infection, which serve as so many damps to the pursuit, a young man that is dependant, having but a small income, will frequently surmount his desires; but when he habituates himself to that destructive vice, the generative organs, by becoming incef-
santly

stantly irritated, bring on a perpetual stimulus, independent of any external cause; so that if there were no more danger to be apprehended from emissions of this kind, than those in the natural way, the train of evils produced by this habit, and the mind being debauched, must demonstrate their fatal tendency; but still more cogent reasons may be adduced, why seminal discharges this way are more destructive than in copulation.

The frequency of erection, though imperfect, which this disposition excites, greatly diminishes the strength of self-polluters. All parts in a state of extention exhaust the powers; the spirits that are conveyed thither in greater quantities, and, of course, dissipated, are wanted in the performance of other functions, which are therefore very imperfectly done; these concurrent causes are

are attended with very dangerous effects. Self-polluters are also afflicted with the palsy in the organs of generation, which brings on impotency, through a defect in erection, and a simple gonorrhœa, by reason of the relaxed parts suffering the real semen to escape as soon as secreted, together with an afflux of that humour which the prostatæ separate. In short, all the internal membrane of the urethra acquires a catarrhous disposition, which excites a running similar to the *fluor albus* in women.

Innumerable are the pores spread over the surface of the human body, which are the emunctories or channels of discharge for vitiated redundancy, or perspirable matter. There also exists on the surface of the body a resorbent faculty. Every instant half the pores of the skin exhale a very subtile humour, that is of greater consequence than

than all our other evacuations. At
the fame time, another kind of pores
receives part of the fluids which furround us, and communicates them to
the veffels. It is demonftrable, that
in fome cafes, this inhalation is very
important. In robuft people, the exhalation is greater than in weak perfons; and, vice verfa, the inhalation
in thefe are more confiderable, and the
perfpiration of healthy people contains
fomething nutritious and ftrengthening,
which being inhaled by another, invigorates him.

From thefe obfervations, we may
draw a conclufion for frequent adoption,
which is by no means uncommon,
but has been practifed time immemorial.
Sacred hiftory has even noticed it in
refpect to David. The exiftence of
aged perfons have been prolonged confiderably by a young perfon, and, confequently,

sequently, it weakens the healthy, who experience a serious loss, without receiving, or rather imbibe weak exhalations, corrupt and putrid, which are highly prejudicial to the constitution.

With respect to seminal discharges by manual friction, and why they are more pernicious in their consequences than the method pointed out by the law of nature, I have already stated. I shall now proceed to the disorders arising from a practice so destructive, and, at the same time, confine myself as much as the nature of the subject will admit, to the horrid victims of self-pollution. The dreadful effects peculiar to the practice cannot be pointed out in colours too expressive, as I consider it an indispensible duty I owe to the public.

The

The general evils which all practitioners who have written upon this subject agree in, are thus specified: the intellectual faculties are weakened, loss of memory ensues, the ideas all clouded, the patient falls sometimes into slight madness, he has an inceffant irksome uneasiness, continual anguish, sight, hearing, and senses deranged, sleep is attended with horrid dreams, the intellectual powers of the body decay, the adoption of it in young persons prevent their growth, hypochondriac and hysteric affections, are the constant attendants, and to draw a conclusion, the whole train of nervous disorders originates from the practice; head-ach is always the consequence, breast, stomach, and intestines, affected, external rheumatic pains, numbness in all parts of the body, when they are slightly pressed; pimples do not only appear in the face, being one of the most common symptoms, but also

also suppurating blisters upon the nose, the breast, and the thighs, painful itching, and even excrescences on the forehead. The organs of generation also participate of that misery whereof they are the primary cause. Many are incapable of erection, others discharge semen upon the slightest titillation, and the most feeble erection, or in efforts when they are at stool. Many are affected with a constant gonorrhœa, which entirely destroys the powers of action, and the discharge resembles fœtid matter, or mucus. Others are subject to priapisms, dysuriœ, stranguries, heat of urine, and a difficulty of discharge. Painful tumours upon the penis, testicles, bladder, and spermatic cord are generally experienced, so that either the impracticability of coition, or a deprivation of the genital liquor, renders every one impotent, who has given way to this practice any length of time. Moreover, the

functions

functions of the intestines are sometimes very much disordered; and some patients complain very much of stubborn constipations, others of the hemorrhoids, or of the running of a fœtid matter from the anus, particularly diarrhœas immediately after the crime.

CASES.

Examples of the wonderful Efficacy of the Nervous Cordial, when administered to relieve the ill Consequences of that truly detestable Sin, SELF POLLUTION.

To WILLIAM BRODUM, M. D.
Author of " The GUIDE TO OLD AGE."

When an individual has experienced any particular mark of kindness, in which his welfare and happiness have been considerably promoted, nothing is more natural than to seek out the person by whom we have been served, for the purpose of expressing our grateful sense of the favour bestowed.

" But

"But in cases of health, where we have been recovered from the last deplorable stage of debilitated nature, and restored to the full enjoyment of all the various blessings of life, we are forcibly called on, by every consideration, to acknowledge it in the most public manner. We owe this equally to our own feelings, which must be sensibly awakened on the occasion, to the skill and talents of the doctor, which merit every encomium, and to the public at large, in order that those who may stand in need of similar benefits, may know where to receive them.

"Having made these general observations, I shall proceed to state the particular case that has occasioned them, and to lay before the public the salutary effects that I have experienced under the greatest afflictions that can possibly befall us.

"I was born and educated at *Winchester*, and at seventeen years of age went to the university at *Oxford*. Prior to my leaving *Winchester*, and more particularly at college, I was reduced to the most grievous state, by these horrid and unnatural practices, too incident to youth, and which are not more baneful to our health, than sinful in the eye of God.

"I was at first afflicted with a dimness of sight, a weakness in my loins, and a depression of spirits. In this situation I applied to Baron *Wenfel*, the famous occulist, who informed me that it proceeded from the optic nerves. I for some time followed his advice, till returning one day from shooting, I was seized with a numbness in my limbs, to such a degree as to lead me to conclude, that I should entirely lose the use of them. This induced me to put myself under the hands of Doctor *W.* of *Oxford,* but neither his aid, nor the waters at *Bath,* which place I visited, afforded me the least relief; my spirits at length were so seriously depressed, with violent palpitations of the heart, and my flesh so much decayed, that I became a mere skeleton. Observing, however, in the *Bath* papers, a publication by Dr. Brodum, intituled, " A Guide to Old Age," dedicated to his Majesty, I was induced to peruse the same, when I prudently discovered the complaint I had so long laboured under.

" I have the happiness to add, that by following the advice contained therein, and going through a complete course of Dr. Brodum's invaluable Nervous Cordial, I am now, thank heaven, perfectly recovered, and as well as ever I was in my life.

" I have since quitted the university, and am going to enter into the holy state of matrimony, with a determination never to be without a " Guide to Old Age ;" and, at the same time, I think it my duty to advise all young men to follow my example, as a perusal of this excellent book may happily prevent the afflicted from being precipitated headlong to an untimely grave, which, but for Dr. Brodum, would most inevitably have been my case.

I am, Sir, yours, &c. &c.

Oxford, October 11, 1796. " A. D. M. A."

To

To Dr. BRODUM.

SIR,

Having in my youth, I confess it with shame, been subject to the heinous offence of Self Pollution, I brought upon myself a running, which neither the cold bath, or any thing that I was advised to apply, could ever remove. Thus circumstanced, no one suspected me of labouring under any bodily complaint, but my doctor, which I account for from being naturally robust, and always preserving my colour. At this crisis I was induced to pay my addresses to a young lady of great personal accomplishments, and soon obtaining her consent, was united to her in the bands of wedlock. This I must acknowledge was highly imprudent in me, who knew from my debilitated state, that I was utterly incapable of consummating my nuptials. A seminal discharge always preceded a perfect erection, which at first I was weak enough to attribute to a too strong desire of possession, but the same disappointment continuing, I had recourse to drinking, which instead of remedying the evil, only increased it; no kind of erection could I procure, and positively emitted the seed always before any connection took place. The distress of being in this unfortunate predicament was greatly heightened, by the fear that my wife had dropped some hints to my mother, of my incapability of performing matrimonial duty, and I looked upon a divorce as inevitable, when I was advised by a friend, to whom I acquainted my truly critical situation, to purchase some bottles of your Nervous Cordial. The persevering in taking this excellent medicine,

medicine, has given a stamina to my constitution, of which I thought my youthful excesses had entirely bereft me, in about five months it accomplished a cure, and it is with pleasure I inform you, that my wife is pregnant with her first child, of which I believe I should never have been the father, had it not been for so invigorating a preparation as the article in question, which may be actually said to give to debilitated constitutions a new existence. I am with gratitude, for the great assistance you have rendered me,

Dear Sir,

Your obedient humble servant.

DEAR SIR, *Portsmouth.*

My situation for many years past has been so truly miserable, that I have often wished for death to relieve me, but I have wished in vain. Owing to juvenile indiscretions, habits contracted at school, I laboured under almost a total deprivation of sight; my memory had lost its retentive powers, and my other faculties were so much impaired, that I had little hopes, while my existence might be prolonged, of being any thing else than a drone in the great hive of society. I had applied to a number of eminent physicians, whose prescriptions, instead of relieving, tended only to increase the malady, until about fourteen months since, I was made acquainted with your truly vauable Nervous Cordial, and after taking three bottles, I

found

found myself so much invigorated, both corporeally and mentally, that I could scarce credit the evidence of my own senses.

By taking two bottles more I found myself so perfectly restored to health and spirits, that I feel myself, if I may be allowed the expression, an inhabitant of another world. About ten months since, I married, and three weeks ago my wife presented me with a son, to the great joy of myself and friends, who have a long time despaired of having the family name perpetuated.

If, Sir, you think the publication of this remarkable case will be a benefit to the community, and to young men in particular, you are perfectly at liberty to do it. My rank and situation in life, make it improper for my name to appear at the bottom of an advertisement, in a public paper. However, I shall be in London, about the middle of next month, when I shall be happy to assure you with what respect and gratitude I am,

Dear Sir,

Your most obliged, humble servant,

W. E. Royal Navy.

A patient applied to me a few months since, out of Lincolnshire, for some of my Nervous Cordial, whose name I suppress from a motive of delicacy, who, by giving way to the enormous and self-punished sin of Onanism, had produced a most sad derangement in the nervous system, accompanied with weakness, uneasiness, weariness, and anxiety. The excessive flux of semen, which he continually discharged, always left him in a most exhausted and emaciated state. His countenance presented a cadaverous appearance, those motions that were easy and natural to others, were difficult and almost impossible for him to perform, his legs would scarcely support him, his digestive powers were so impaired, that he could not keep his food above three or four hours upon his stomach, and the multiplicity of phlegm that he expectorated, was to him a source of pain and anxietude.

In this perturbid state of mind, and debilitated system of body, I administered to him my Nervous Cordial, which considering the multiplicity of his complaints, and his irresolution for some time to discontinue a practice that had involved him in such complicated distresses, effected wonders. He has now become hale and robust, and earnestly laments his having so long given way to a vice so fraught with danger and self-destruction, as the sin of Onanism.

Habits of this pernicious nature have been known to be used by children, at the early period of from eight to ten years of age, one of which in particular came under my own cognizance.

A youth

A youth at this tender period of life indulged himself in this pernicious practice, which so much impaired his constitution, that his nerves became exceedingly weak, his hands lost their strength, inceſſant tremblings agitated every atom of his frame, he was always in a state of perspiration, he had constantly pains in the stomach, and alternately in every part of his arms, legs, breast, and veins. A cough was always the companion of these symptoms, his aspect became cadaverous, his legs fell away to a shadow, and his appetite was so destroyed, as seldom to induce him to obey the call of nature. Notwithstanding the existence of these symptoms, the Nervous Cordial soon restored him to his former health and vigour, blessings which he had every reason in the world to believe he should never again experience.

The Doctor has been recently supplied with the two following melancholy catastrophes of persons who have pursued this hateful vice to excess.

A youth about seventeen devoted himself to this seductive practice so entirely, that he would repeat the act three or four times in one day, which was both preceded and succeeded by insensibility, and attended by a swelling in the neck, and convulsive motion in the extending muscles of the head. After continuing this vice some months he became exceedingly feeble, but nevertheless persisted until he came to death's door, when the evil had made such a progress, that no medicine could afford him the least relief. His organs of generation were so weakened, that his semen flowed involuntarily from him on the slightest erection.

tion. An habitual spasm, which at first only affected him in the very act, now continued for twelve or fourteen hours at a time, which produced such violent pains in the neck, that the most alarming outcries were the consequence. At these junctures he could not swallow any food, and after languishing for many months, he died the most pitiable object perhaps that ever fell a victim to disease.

Before his death he more resembled a corpse than a living man, and the infectious effluvia that came from every part of his deceased body, was shocking beyond comparison. His mind was as disordered as his body, and his memory so impaired, that he could not retain the least idea of any thing but a knowledge of his own pain.

Boerhaave mentions another patient, who, through the adoption of this predominant passion, was first afflicted with a stiffness in the neck, which communicated to the spine, and afterwards to the other members. The inveteracy of this complaint soon compleated his dissolution, but before he died he could not bear himself in any other posture than lying on his belly in bed, without being able to use his hands or feet, or take any sustenance into his mouth. He existed in this lamentable situation several weeks.

These cases are introduced to shew the danger that arises to youth, from exercising passions that are a disgrace to human nature.

An

An inftance occurred to me a few days fince. A captain from the Eaft Indies being on the point of marriage, who laboured under a dreadful confumption, and was apprehenfive matrimonial engagements would be detrimental to the reftoration of his health, informed me, that, previous to his going to the Indies, he had been injured by the Venereal Difeafe, and at the time of his applying to me, was under the direction of an eminent phyfician, but found himfelf every day weaker and more relaxed. After a ftrict examination, I found not the leaft fymptom of a venereal taint, which induced me to enforce the queftion to him, whether he had ever been addicted to that baneful habit, to which he candidly acknowledged he had. I recommended to him the Nervous Cordial, which he took for fix weeks, and is now perfectly reftored.

CHAP.

CHAP. XXII.

ON THE FEMALE SEX.

WITH the most heartfelt regret I am under the indispensable necessity of observing, that the tender sex, the most amiable part of the creation, those for whom we are animated to glory, danger, and every enterprise which we think will recommend us to their regard; that these desirable objects, who should obey the dictates of nature, and render our passions and our loves congenial, have their minds as well as bodies frequently enervated by shameful practices, which they are so silly as to
im-

imagine are entirely hidden from the world; but which are but too plainly depicted in their countenances, and by their frigid relish for genuine love, and their unnatural diftafte to the male part of the creation, for whom they were by Providence deftined; for their bodies are by thefe filthy practices not only fo weakened and emaciated, that they are often rendered barren, and thereby greatly prejudice fociety and pofterity; but they at length contract an unconquerable habit of this kind of gratification, which is always fo ready at hand, and which they fancy an indulgence, without the danger of child-bearing, the lofs of reputation, or of health. In this they greatly deceive themfelves; for the evil confequences of fuch practices are infinitely more dreadful than any of the dangers which terrify them from natural enjoyment.

This

This it muſt be owned is a delicate point to treat upon; and it may be urged in their defence, that ſtrong paſſions, a naturally amorous conſtitution are great palliatives for what they may think an innocent amuſement. Parents and relations, who ſuperintend their introduction into life, do not conſider how early theſe natural operations take place; that if they are thinking of a huſband for a daughter, they are conſulting rather the force of his pocket, than the ſtrength of his conſtitution, and the riſk a young woman is liable to, in having intercourſe with a man before marriage. It were to be wiſhed, that parents would conſult the real happineſs of their children, and not attempt to curb thoſe deſires that are not only laudable when directed in a proper channel, but rather endeavours to promote their gratification as far as they are reaſonable. To this end, it would be prudent to provide a proper huſband for

for a daughter as soon as she is marriageable, instead of permitting her to languish till she is five or six and twenty in hopes of a good match. Mothers should not attempt to persuade daughters that they are mere children when they are as capable of being mothers as themselves, with no other view than that their real age may not be guessed at or discovered. Such artifices as these are constantly detected; and it would be much more to their credit to be young gran-dames than old coquettes.

The females of England and other northern climates, do not attain the age of maturity so early as in more southern latitudes. In Asia, women are almost past child-bearing as early as some cold constitutions in the northern parts of America have little more than attained the age of puberty. But in general, females in England are capable of childbearing about fifteen; and this is teftified by the marks of puberty, the projection of their breafts, and monthly purgations. Many have thefe figns at thirteen and fourteen, and confequently could increafe our progeny from that time, till about the age of forty-five, which is the period when women in this part of the world ufually difcontinue the menfes, and are paft childbearing. It muft therefore be very impolitic for a ftate to prevent a female being able to difpofe of her perfon in wedlock till fhe arrives at twenty-one, fince, it is evident, fhe might in that time have produced fix or feven fubjects, the number of which conftitute the moft permanent riches, profperity, and fecurity of a kingdom.

Thus much I have faid to palliate, if poffible, any errors in the conduct of the ladies,

ladies, whose advocate I would willingly be upon every occasion; but let not any female imagine, that the most elaborate eloquence can ever excuse their pursuing this abominable practice, which is more baneful, as it may be said to be contagious, a single sinner, in this respect, having frequently corrupted a whole seminary of virtuous girls.

With regard to maids who have hereby deprived themselves of that sacred badge, the loss of which before marriage was so severely punished by the Jews; under what apprehensions must they continually lie, with what terrors they approach the marriage bed which heaven has designed for the seat of the highest sensible enjoyment, when they reflect that their virtue, on the first amorous encounter, is liable to such suspicions, as may never be worn off, but which may render uncomfortable the whole life both of her and her otherwife affectionate hufband. May not thefe reflections make fuch an impreffion on fome as to hinder them from entering on a ftate to which they are warmly folicited, and which nature prompts them to defire, for fear of a detection which would turn fo greatly to their difquiet. I much doubt if there have not been many old maids on no other account than this.

The danger to which women expofe themfelves by fo deftructive a gratification of their paffions, are very analagous to thofe which men are liable to from this filthy practice. The humour which is loft by females is not, it is true, fo elaborate as the male femen, and may not therefore enfeeble the body fo fpeedily; but when they are guilty of exceffes, their nervous fyftem being weaker than ours, and naturally more liable to fpafms,

the

the accidents arifing therefrom are ftill more evident: they alfo are expofed to hyfterical fits, and dreadful vapours; to incurable jaundices; to violent cramps in the ftomach and back; to acute pains in the nofe; to the fluor albus, the acreation whereof is a continual fource of the moft fmarting pain; to defcents and ulcerations of the matrix, and to all the infirmities which thefe diforders bring on; to the furor uterinus, which at once deprives them of decency and reafon, a ftate in which they cannot long exift, as their vices and crimes, when arrived at this extreme, muft foon terminate their exiftence.

A fine woman, in the beft ftate of health, who addicts herfelf to this direful practice, will experience an early decay of her charms, her eyes will lofe their luftre, and become languid and dead, her complexion fade, her ftrength experience

rience a rapid decline, and in a fhort time, if fhe perfeveres in the habit, from an agreeable and defirable object, fhe will become not only difagreeable to the men, but even difguftful to herfelf; and if it is true, as Rochefoucalt fays, that the laft fighs of a fine woman are more for the lofs of her beauty than her life, fhe will have the irkfome talk of anticipating this mortification in the very prime of youth. We are told by all the profeffors who have written upon this fubject, that young people of either fex, who addict themfelves to it, fall away and diminifh, inftead of increafing in their growth; and we often find young people of both fexes, but particularly females, who, being well made at the age of ten or twelve, become afterwards crooked, by bending and weaknefs of the fpine.

I have

I have already mentioned the disgust that is created by this practice to natural pleasures, and it is still stronger in females than in our sex; for women, who have habituated themselves to this practice, are always indifferent to the lawful duties of the conjugal bed, when their inclinations and power still remain, and this indifference does not only induce many females to embrace a life of celibacy, but accompanies others who have been prevailed upon to enter into the married state, and we have testimonies of many females, with whom this practice had gained so complete a dominion over their senses, that they held in detestation that great law of nature pointed out by the omnipotent Creator of the universe.

CASES.

CASES.

A young lady of Birmingham, who was long afflicted, and whose disorder was considered a decline, was advised by her friends to go to Manchester, and have the advice of that eminent physician Dr. Percival; the doctor's opinion was, that she was not in a decline, but her complaint proved of so precarious a nature as to baffle that eminent physician, as well as many others, consulted prior to her applying to him. She at length became so weak and emaciated, as to be incapable of walking across the room, and at last unable to rise from the chair without assistance. Still growing worse, she was prevailed upon, though with great difficulty, owing to her continual pains and weak state, to make trial of a journey to London, to consult another eminent physician, Dr. Pitcairn, when after seeing her in the wretched state she appeared in, and considering medical assistance vain, was candid enough to say he could render her no service; fortunately, a lady of her acquaintance, who had been in a decline, and had been recovered by the advice of, and taking Dr. Brodum's Nervous Cordial, strongly recommended her to consult the doctor, and to disclose her case in as clear and open a manner as she possibly could, the which she was prevailed upon by sending her nurse, who was her confidant, to the doctor, at his house, who, after hearing the nurse, conjectured she might be rather diffident in disclosing her disorder, as far as she knew of it, and by pressing her not to deceive him, but to open the cafe in as clear a manner as fhe could, fhe confeffed fhe had been guilty of this deftructive practice nine years; the doctor accordingly treated her as fuch, when to the utmoft aftonifhment of all who knew her, by taking two five guinea bottles of Dr. Brodum's Nervous Cordial, and ftrictly adhering to his advice, fhe was perfectly reftored to her former ftate of health, in four months, has fince married, and been bleffed with two children.

A young lady of family and fortune, whofe diforder was treated as a cancer, which in fact was not, it being an inflammation brought on by the above practice, and through the very great danger of the complaint, and the wifh of being reftored, fhe was prevailed on by the intreaties of a favoured fervant, at the inftance of the mother, to own her indifcretion, and difcover the real caufe of her complaint; fhe acknowledged being addicted to that pernicious habit for feveral years, by being initiated to that practice at a boarding fchool. By my advice fhe took the Nervous Cordial, ufed fomentations, and was in two months recovered to perfect health.

A married woman caufed her cafe to be made known to me, through the channel of her midwife, which was nearly as as follows: "When I was a young girl, at the age of fourteen or fifteen, being enticed by some of my school-fellows, and particularly my bed-fellow, I began to penetrate those parts, which should never have been explored but by a husband. This practice I continued till I was run away with by a music-master, at eighteen; it were needless to enumerate the difficulties I met with till my relations were reconciled to the match. Sufficient it is to say, I had four children by my husband in three years, two being twins, but they all died; and also my husband soon after. I was in a state of widowhood for three years, and then married again, with the approbation of my relations. Before this union, I found all my girlish inclinations come upon me, and not daring to risk any connection with a man, I repeated my former practice with such violence, (particularly just before and after my monthly courses) that I made myself violently sore; and brought on such a bearing down of the womb, that it was with much difficulty I could walk. These complaints have increased since my last marriage; and though four years have elapsed from that period, I have not been once pregnant. I had been prevailed upon by my husband to undergo a physician's inspection, prior to my application to Dr. Brodum, when he said that my womb was very weak and slippery, and he was afraid I should never have any more children. He, however, prescribed the Bath water and injections; but they proved of no service, as I continued really weakened, by a white running, which was very considerable, and with the bearing down, which frequently is very great, and occasioned a continual pain in my womb, and in my back, whereby I was greatly

fallen

fallen away; and what is remarkable, I had no manner of inclination for the act of procreation, and very little or no pleasure in the act at all, which I am inclined to believe was as much the reason as any other of my incapacity of bearing children; fortunate for me, having, as before mentioned, made application to Dr. Brodum, I have the satisfaction to say, that in two months, by strictly attending to the prescriptions of Dr. Brodum, and taking his Nervous Cordial, I found a considerable amendment, as the white running has ceased, and my strength amazingly increasing, and have not a doubt, by the blessing of God, and Dr. Brodum's assistance, of being completely restored in a short time to a good state of health."

———

A married woman, aged about forty-seven years, consulted me for barrenness, from a laxness of muscular fibres of the vagina and uterus; but examining the case, and suspecting both from the character she bore, and from what she herself had said, that it was not owing to any insufficiency in the husband, whom she publicly complained of, but to her own insatiable lust; for it plainly appeared her case was owing to friction; wherefore, considering her age, and the little hopes of success, I declined saying any thing upon the subject; however the same woman, without my knowledge, began taking my Nervous Cordial, which she strictly adhered to, according to the directions given with each bottle, when by taking the same for three months, she

she found a wonderful alteration in her whole frame for the better, which induced her to wait again upon me, and relate the resolution she had formed of a trial of the Nervous Cordial; and further requested me to give her other advice towards re-establishing her to her former state. I gave her a prescription, and desired her to continue the Cordial, which she did for at least four months more, when she has informed me she considered herself perfectly restored, and as hearty in every respect as ever she was in her life.

CHAP.

CHAP XXIII.

Of the Diforders incident to the Female Sex, and the moſt approved Methods of Cure.

AFTER what has been faid concerning the filthy, ſhameful, and deſtructive practices of the women, by themſelves, or amongſt each other, which occafions fuch a variety of evils and diforders, it were but juſtice to the fex to own, that, from their natural formation and difpofition, and the incidental cafualties attending pregnancy and child-bearing, they are fubject to many afflictions in various refpects, analogous to thofe mentioned in former fections, sections, and from which the men are entirely exempted; and therefore I think it neceſſary to explain myſelf upon theſe heads in this ſection.

The whites are a foul excretion from the womb, commonly attendant upon weak women, oftentimes after hard labour, ſometimes during pregnancy, and frequently in a virgin ſtate. This diſorder is a diſtillation of a variety of corrupt humours through the womb, flowing from different parts of the body. This oozing is of many colours, ſometimes black, yellow, green, red, and blue. Having no periodical flux, as the regular menſes, its returns are diſorderly and uncertain.

The cauſe of this diſorder may be attributed to a general weakneſs, or cacochymia, and ſometimes to a partial debility, as in the liver, which, by the

inability

inability of the fanguificative faculty, occafions a generation of corrupt blood; in this cafe, the matter is reddifh, when the gall is remifs in its office, not drawing away the choleric fuperfluities which are engendered in the liver, when the fpleen does not fufficiently perform its office, in cleanfing the blood of the dregs and excrementitious parts, it then is blackifh; fometimes it is occafioned by catarrhs in the head, or from any other member that is in a difordered ftate; when the flowing is whitifh, the caufe refides in the reins or the ftomach; if in the reins, it is occafioned by being over-heated, which caufes the fpermatic matter, by reafon of its tenuity, to flow involuntarily; but when the ftomach is the feat of the complaint, it is occafioned by crude and vitiated matter remaining there undigefted, by reafon of melancholy, or fome ftomachic complaints, and this vitiated matter is communicated to the womb by the liver, or inftead of being appropriated to chyle; if the diforder proceed from crudities in the ftomach, or from a cold difordered liver, take every morning a decoction of lignum quafliæ (which is highly recommended by that eminent phyfician Dr. Lettfom) and half a drachm of pil-ruffi, a fcruple of aloes, fyrup of ginger, fufficient to make up twelve pills, of which take two every night; but particularly let the womb be cleanfed from corrupt matter, and be ftrengthened; for the cleanfing whereof, make injections of mugwort, fpikenard, biftort, mercury, all of which may be got at an herb-ftall, fage, adding thereto fugar, oil of fweet almonds, of each an ounce. The womb fhould be ftrengthened, for which you may ufe fomentations made of red wine, after maftich, fine bole, baluftia, and red rofes; and to take of the NERVOUS CORDIAL four tea-fpoon fulls, twice each

each day; the beſt is a dry regimen; this diſtemper being occaſioned by phlegmatic and crude humours; too much ſleep is alſo pernicious, and, on the other hand, moderate exerciſe is eligible.

I have been the more circumſtantial in preſcribing for the cure of this diſorder, as it is more general than may be thought, and is, indeed, concomitant with a weak or over delicate conſtitution; therefore, ladies of this complexion ſhould pay the greateſt attention to remove the complaint before it makes too great a progreſs. To this end, I would have every female, who finds herſelf ſubject to this affliction, examine ſtrictly, whether or not her ſuſpicions are well founded, and to keep the parts particularly clean, by waſhing with lukewarm water, at leaſt every other day. Beſides the ſatisfaction it muſt afford every female to know the real ſituation of her own body, and, if difordered, timely to remedy it; there is nothing which is more productive of health in this refpect, and, as a proof of it, an additional gratification will arife therefrom in the act of copulation, and it will greatly tend to the improvement of their complexion.

The diforders relative to the monthly courfes are fo very analogous to the former, that many have called the whites the falfe courfes, though, in fact, they arife from a different fource. Nature has made provifion for the nourifhment of children during their recefs in the womb of their mother, by that redundancy of blood, which is natural to all women, and which flowing out at certain periods of time, when they are not pregnant, are from thence called terms and menfes, from their monthly flux of excrementitious and unprofitable blood.

As

As to this flux being excrementitious, is to be underſtood only with regard to the redundancy and overplus of it, as it is in no other way an excrement, than with reſpect to quantity, being, in point of quality, as pure and incorrupt as any blood in the veins; and this appears by its final deſtination, the propagation and conſervation of mankind, as alſo by its generation, being the ſuperfluity of the laſt aliment of the fleſhy parts. Theſe monthly purgations uſually commence about the fourteenth year, and continue to the forty-fifth, but not without frequent intervening ſuppreſſions, which are ſometimes natural, and ſometimes morbific: they are natural in pregnant women, and thoſe who give ſuck; but when morbific, they are occaſioned by an interruption of that accuſtomary evacuation of blood which ſhould monthly flow from the matrix, and which proceed from the matter being vitiated: the

the cauſe is, in this caſe, either internal or external; the internal cauſe, either inſtrumental or material, in the blood, or in the womb. The blood may be faulty two ways, in quantity or in quality; in quantity, when it is ſo conſumed that there is not an overplus left, as in viragoes, and all other virile women, who, through their heat and ſtrength of nature, digeſt and conſume all their beſt nouriſhment: The blood may alſo be conſumed, and the terms ſuppreſſed by too much bleeding at the noſe; likewiſe by a flux of the hemorrhoids, by a dyſenteria, evacuations, chronical and continual diſorders: and the matter may alſo be vicious in quality, as when ſanguineous, phlegmatical, bilious, or melancholic; each of theſe, if they offend in groſſneſs, will cauſe an obſtruction in the veins. The defect may likewiſe, for various reaſons, reſide in the womb, as, by the narrowneſs of the veins and paſſages

passages by aposthumes, tumours, ulcers, and by over much cold and heat, the one vitiating the action, the other consuming the matter; also by an evil composition of the matter; also by an evil composition of the uterine parts, by the neck of the womb being turned aside, and sometimes, though but rarely, by a membrane or excrescence of flesh growing about the womb: The external cause may be heat or dryness of the air, immoderate walking, great labour, violent motion, whereby the matter is so consumed, and the body is so exhausted, that there is no redundant blood remaining to be expelled; whence it is recorded of the Amazons, that being active, and always in motion, they had little or no monthly fluxes. It may also be caused by cold, and most frequently is so, the blood being thereby rendered vicious and gross, condensing and binding up the passages, that it cannot flow forth. If the suppression be natural, and caused by by corruption, it may be known by drinking honey and water after supper, on going to bed; for if, after taking it, the woman feel a bearing pain about the navel, and the lower parts of the belly, it is a sign she has conceived, and that the suppression is natural. If she does not find this effect from drinking the honey and water, she may conclude it to be vitious, and should immediately endeavour to promote the return of the menses, in the manner hereafter prescribed, otherwise the effects may be very dangerous, as this suppression may occasion swimmings, faintings, intermission of pulse, obstructions, chachexies, jaundice, dropsies, hardness of the spleen, epilepsies, apoplexies, phrensy, &c. Evacuations are, in this case, proper, and therefore, in the middle of the menstrual period, it will be proper to open the liver vein; and, for the reversion of the humour, two days after the evacuation,

evacuation, open the faphena vein of both feet, and, if the repletion be not great, apply cupping glaffes to the legs and thigh. After phlebotomy, the humours muft be prepared, and made flexible with fyrup of ftæchas, horehound, hyfop, betony, maidenhair, mugwort, and fumitory; then let a bath be made of rue, fetherfew, marjorum, favin, bay leaves, penny royal, camomile, and juniper berries; after which take of the leaves of nop and maidenhair, each one handful, make a decoction, of which take three ounces; fyrup of mugwort and maidenhair, mix of each half an ounce, and when the patient comes out of the bath, let her drink it all. Galen, in this cafe, commends pilula de hiera cum colycintida, as being proper to purge the offending humour; they are calculated to open the paffages of the womb; if the patient's ftomach be overcharged, let her take

take a vomit; but let it be prepared in such manner as to operate also as a cathartic, left the humours should be too much turned back, by working only upwards; wherefore, take of trochiscs of agaric two drachms, infuse them in three ounces of oximel, in which dissolve benedict. laxat. half an ounce, and of the electuary of diasarum, one scruple, which is to be taken as a purgative. When the humour hath, in this manner, been purged, more efficacious and forcible remedies may be applied, such as the extract of mugwort, one scruple and a half, musk ten grains, trochiscs of myrrh, one drachm and a half, rinds of caffia, parsley seed, castor, of each one scruple, to be taken with the juice of orange, on going to bed. The lower parts should also be administered to by fumigation, pessaries, unctions, injections, and inseffions: make suffumigations of amber, galbanum, bay berries,

berries, mugwort, cinnamon, nutmegs, cloves, &c. make peſſaries of figs, and the leaves of mercury, bruiſed, and rolled up with lint; make injections of the decoctions of mercury, betony, origin, mugwort, and figs, and inject it into the womb with a ſponge. For unction, take ladant, oil of myrrh, of each two drachms; oil of lilies, almonds, capers, camomile, of each half an ounce; and with wax, make an unguent to anoint the place.

The patient ſhould alſo remain in a dry warm air; ſhould not ſleep much; but, on the other hand, ſhe ſhould uſe moderate exerciſe, eſpecially before meals, which ſhould conſiſt of attenuating food; take alſo four teaſpoonfuls of the Nervous Cordial twice a day, with a glaſs of red wine after each.

The overflowing of the menses, is a disorder directly opposite to that which I have just been speaking of. This complaint is a sanguineous excrement, consisting of blood, and proceeding from the womb, and exceeding in time and quality. The cause of this overflowing is either external or internal. The external cause may be the heat of the air, the lifting or carrying heavy burthens, unnatural child-births, falls, &c. The internal cause may be threefold: in the matter, instrument, or faculty; the matter, which is the blood, may be vitious, two ways: First, in quantity, being so much, that the veins are not able to contain it: Secondly, in quality, being adust, sharp, or unconcocted. The instrument, that is to say, the veins, are faulty, by the dilatation of the orifice, which may be caused two ways, by the heat of the constitution, climate, or season, heating the blood, whereby the

passages

paſſages are dilated, and the faculty ſo much weakened, that it cannot retain the blood. Secondly, by falls, blows, violent motions, breaking of veins, &c. If it comes by the breaking of a vein, the body is ſometimes cold, the blood flows forth in heaps, and that ſuddenly accompanied with great pain. If it be occaſioned by heat, the orifice of the veins being dilated, there is little or no pain attending it, yet the blood flows faſter than it doth in an eroſion, and not ſo faſt as in a rupture. If it ariſe from an eroſion or ſharpneſs of blood, ſhe feels a great ſcalding in the paſſage; and in this caſe it differs from the other two, in its flowing not ſo ſuddenly nor ſo copiouſly as in thoſe; if it be occaſioned by the weakneſs of the womb, ſhe has an averſion to copulation, even in the very act. If it proceed from the blood, drop ſome of it on a cloth, and when it is dry, the quality may be judged from the

the colour; when choleric, it will be yellowifh; if melancholy, blackifh, phlegmatic, waterifh, and whitifh. The cure of this complaint confifts in three things: Firft, the repelling and carrying back the blood; fecondly, the correcting and taking away the fluxibility of the matter; and thirdly, the corroborating the veins or faculties. In the firft cafe, to promote a regreffion of the blood, phlebotomy in the arm will be ufeful, and fuch a quantity of blood may be taken away, as the ftrength of the patient will permit, which, however, fhould not be done at once, but at different periods, the fpirits being thereby lefs weakened, and the retraction fo much the greater. The cupping-glafs fhould be applied to the liver, that the reverfion may be in the fountain moderated with cathartics; it is neceffary to correct the fluxibility of the matter. When it is occafioned by the acrimony of of the blood, it should be considered whether the erosion be by salt phlegm, or of a dust colour; if by the first, prepare wormwood, rosin, citron-peel, with syrup of violets; mild purgatives should also be taken, and make a decoction in plaintain water, adding thereto syrup rosæ. lax. three ounces, to make a potion. When by adust colour, prepare the body with syrup of roses; myrtles, sorrel, and purslain, mixed with plaintain water; and then, two days following, to take four tea-spoonfuls twice a day. If the blood flows from the breaking of a vein, without any evil quality of itself, strengtheners only in this case should be applied; for which purpose a scruple of bole armoniac, a drachm of treacle, half an ounce of conserve of roses, with syrup of myrtle, make an excellent electuary. In case the flux is of long continuance, two drachms of mastich, a drachm of olibanum, and an ounce

ounce of troch de careble, with one
fcruple of baluftium, made into powder,
and with. the fyrup of quinces, formed
into pills, will be falutary.

There is another diforder attending
the menfes, which is their irregularity.
When they come before their time, there
is a depraved excretion, which often
fupplies their place at the expected periods; and, in this cafe, they return
twice a month. The caufe, in this cafe,
refides in the blood, which ftirs up the
expulfive faculty in the womb, and,
fometimes, in the whole body, and is
frequently occafioned by the patient's
diet, which increafing the blood too
much, renders it too fharp or too hot;
and, in cafe the retentive faculty of the
womb be weak, and the expulfive faculty ftrong, and of a quick fenfe, they
are brought forth the fooner by means
of a fall, a blow, or fome violent paf-
fion,

sion, which the person afflicted can account for; if it be occasioned by heat, thin and sharp humours, the whole body is disordered. It is, in this case, more troublesome than dangerous, but is pernicious to conception. If it arise from the sharpness of the blood, good diet, the Nervous Cordial, and bathing at Tunbridge Wells, will be necessary. If the blood be thick and foul, it should be thinned, and the humours mixed therewith be evacuated, wherefore it is proper to take purgatives after the courses, and to use calamints, fumes, pessaries, and the application of cupping-glasses without; scarification to the inside of the thighs, is also necessary; the legs should likewise be rubbed, the ancles scarified, and the feet held in warm water, four or five days before the courses come down; proper applications are also necessary to be made to the pudendum, in order to provoke the flowing of the menses,

menses, some time before they are expected.

The last disorder which I shall mention, peculiar to the women, is the falling of the womb, which is not only extremely troublesome, but is also a hindrance to conception. The womb will sometimes descend as low as her knees. This is occasioned by the ligaments, which unite it to the other parts being out of order. There are four ligaments, two above, broad and membraneous, which come from the peritonæum, and two below, which are nervous, round, and hollow. The womb is also bound to the great vessels by veins and arteries, and to the back by nerves. The womb changes its place, when it is drawn another way, and when the ligaments are loose, its own weight bears it down. It is drawn on one side when the menstruum are hindered from flowing, and the

the veins and arteries which go to the womb are full. If there be a *mole**, on one fide the liver and the fpleen will caufe it, the liver veins on the right fide, and the fpleen on the left, being more or lefs replenifhed.

---

* A mole is a falfe conception, or lump of flefh, burthening in the womb. Some are of opinion, that it is produced from the woman's feed going into the womb without the man's; but this can only mean, if any thing, that fome of the ova having gained admittance into the womb, by mafturbation, or fome fuch filthy practice. Other phyficians are of opinion, that it is engendered of the menftruous. blood; but in this cafe, it would follow, that maids, by having their courfes ftopped, would be fubject to this accident; but this has never yet been proved. The real caufe of this carnous conception proceeds both from the man and the woman; from corrupt and barren feed in the man, and from the menftruous blood in the woman, both mingled together in the cavity of the womb, and nature finding herfelf weak, yet endeavouring to maintain the perpetuity of her fpecies, labours to bring forth fuch a vicious conception, rather than none, and, being incapable of producing a living creature, generates a lump of flefh.

Some phyficians are of opinion, that this diforder arifes from the folution of the connection of the febinous neck, and the parts adjacent: be this as it may, with women in the dropfy the falling of the womb is occafioned by the faltnefs of the water. When there is a little tumour, like the fkin ftretched, within or without the pudendum, or a weight felt about the privities, thefe are fymptoms of the falling of the womb. When there is a tumour like a goofe's egg, and a hole at the bottom, great pain is at firft felt in the parts to which the womb is faftened, fuch as the loins, the bottom of the belly, and the os facrum, which is occafioned by the breaking or ftretching of the ligaments. Fomentations of red wine, boiled with flor-balauftin, fhould be applied, as it tends greatly to ftrengthen the weakened parts; bandages alfo for the purpofe, to be had at the Doctor's houfe; four tea-fpoonfuls

fuls of the Nervous Cordial should be taken four times a day.

But those cases are, in general, of so dangerous a nature, as to require the personal attendance of the Doctor.

CHAP.

CHAP. XXIV.

A Sovereign Plaſter for the Diſorders of the Matrix, &c.

OF cerus, a quarter of a pound; minium, half a pound; Genoa ſoap, five ounces; oil of olives, one pound; put the minium and the cerus in a pan upon the fire; continue ſtirring the ſame, till they are well incorporated and united together; then cut the ſoap in ſmall bits, and put it in piece by piece, keeping the contents of the pan continually ſtirring; let it do over a middling fire, till ſuch time as it become grey, or a cheſnut colour; take care that nothing boils over, whilſt it is boiling, as theſe ingredients ſwell a good

good deal, and continue conſtantly ſtirring till it be boiled enough; when it is of a good conſiſtence, take it off the fire, and ſtir it till it be cold, when rolls are to be made of it; and care muſt be taken not to handle them with wet hands.

When there is occaſion to uſe this plaſter, it muſt be ſpread upon linen or leather; but if upon leather, care muſt be taken that it has no ſcent.

If the ligaments of the womb are relaxed, and a bearing down enſues, it ſhould be applied to the navel, the patient remaining in bed two days, and keeping it on till ſuch time as ſhe be cured. It ſhould, however, be taken off at the end of a fortnight, the place wiped, and another plaſter put on, remaining without any bandage.

If a woman, when brought to bed, has any difficulty of having the after-birth brought away, this plaster will be greatly efficacious in performing it, by being put upon the navel, and leaving it in the manner above prescribed.

If a lying-in woman, or any other, or a maid, has too great a flux of the menses, this is a sovereign remedy, by applying it to the navel, as above.

If a woman, or a young girl, has not a sufficient flux of her monthly courses, or there is an entire suppression of them, this plaster should be used; and, in this case, it should be placed beneath the navel.

CHAP.

THIS infectious diforder was brought into Europe, according to the beft authorities, from America, by the failors who accompanied Columbus on his ever memorable expedition in the year 1493. They communicated it to the Neapolitan women, of whom the French contracted it at the fiege of Naples, from which circumftance it derived the appellation of the French difeafe.

It is denominated a local infection when the venereal contagion has not affected the whole mafs of blood, but is is confined to any particular part. What conftitutes a univerfal infection is when it enters the habit, and affects the fluids.

The Venereal difeafe is communicated almoft imperceptibly through the medium of the genitals, nipples, lips, and any part that is covered by the cuticle. Examining venereal ulcers with cut fingers have frequently produced it with great virulence.

Dr. Smith relates a cafe of a young lady of family and fortune, who contracted a taint of fo fatal a nature as to be the death of her in confequence of her fweetheart's kiffing her when venereal ulcers were formed in his mouth and throat. This is inferted to prove how extremely cautious young perfons fhould be againft innocently catching a diftemper that may, like the example

in

in queftion, injure their reputation, and terminate their life.

Dr. Rutherford, of Edinburgh, fays, that a clap is an internal chancre, though the diffection of bodies demonftrates the contrary.

So fubtle is the poifon of the Venereal Difeafe, that nurfes who have had infants fucking at their breafts, have frequently communicated it through the nipple; how neceffary, therefore, is it for parents to ftudy the morals of thofe to whom they place their children; and, on the other hand, nurfes frequently imbibe the contagion through fuckling infected children.

When this diforder is contracted, the taint is conveyed into the lymphatic glands. From the penis it is communicated to the glands of the corpora cavernofa,

vernofa, the urethra, and afterwards to the inguen. From the nipples to the axillæ.

A gonorrhœa is an inflammation and exoriation of the glands or vagina, and the urethra, in both fexes.

Cleanlinefs, in every fpecies of this complaint, is indifpenfably neceffary for both fexes to obferve. The parts affected fhould be carefully wafhed with warm milk and water, which, by removing the irritating particles, has often, without any other affiftance, cured a fimple gonorrhœa.

The ufe of mercury, as a fpecific in this difeafe, is, by far, too general. When the difeafe is communicated to the fyftem at large, mercurials are, with great propriety, made ufe of both externally and internally; though I much queftion, question, whether ever, in the worſt ſtage of the Venereal Diſeaſe that ever yet exiſted, it was ever neceſſary to produce that complete ſalivation which is ſo generally practiſed in the hoſpitals in this kingdom. And in ſlighter and more local affections, the introduction of mercury into the conſtitution can be productive of no benefit, and is often attended with very great diſadvantage. Much caution, therefore, and the advice of thoſe whom a long experience has rendered capable and ſkillful, is neceſ- ſary in the uſe of this active mineral. The ſame occurs with reſpect to arſenic, which, though in the hands of the vulgar, is often employed as a poiſon to deſtroy life, yet, in the hands of the experienced chemiſt and phyſician, may be converted to the moſt beneficial pur- poſes.

The Arabians were the firſt who in- vented the uſe of this medicine, and embraced

embraced the opportunity, as an excellent means of deſtroying their vermin, which example was followed by Peter, the Spaniard, a celebrated Phyſician, who was created Pope in the year 1726, and took the name of John XXI.

When mercury was firſt adminiſtered for the cure of the Venereal Diſeaſe, it was given with great caution, and attended with the beſt of advice, and was productive of infinite benefit to mankind, but ſince that period, it is difficult to aſcertain whether the good it has effected will counterbalance the innumerable evils an improper uſe has occaſioned.

It is much to be deplored, that the modern ſyſtem of medicine ſhould vary from ancient practice. Formerly, the moſt malignant of diſorders were expelled by the proper applications of roots;

roots; an art that the Americans practise to this day with the greateſt ſuccefs. Nature has given us an antidote for every difeafe, and, for myfelf, I feel happy, that through my knowledge of the vegetable world, I have been able to compoſe a preparation of the moſt ſanative plants, roots, &c. which will effectually eradicate ſo deſtructive and obnoxious a complaint as the Venereal Difeafe.

The Botanical Syrup is compoſed of ſuch innocent ingredients, that inſtead of impairing the conſtitution, as is the cafe in all mercurial preparations, will fortify it with ſtrength, and finally, in the worſt of venereal cafes, will purify the blood, and correct the habit of the body, and ſo remove every ſymptom of that truly horrid but too general complaint.

CASES.

CASES.

I hereby atteſt, that I have been effectually cured by Dr. Brodum, of Albion-ſtreet, Blackfriar's-road, of an inward ſcorbutic complaint, likewiſe a certain diſorder that delicacy forbids me to mention, though moſt of our frail ſex are liable thereto; in the ſmall ſpace of three weeks, notwithſtanding I had received the advice of ſeveral other medical men, and ſtrictly conformed to the rules laid down, but without experiencing the leaſt relief; but providentially applying to Dr. Brodum, as above, by the aſſiſtance of his advice, and taking his Reſtorative Nervous Cordial, I was completely cured in three weeks, as above-mentioned.

No. 5, *Blue Anchor Alley*,   THOMAS NORTON.
Bunhill Row.

Witneſſes—*T. Sabine*, Printer, No. 81, *Shoe Lane*; and *James Salter*, Druggiſt, No. 29, *Poultry*.

N. B. The said *Thomas Norton* ſwore to the truth of the above, this 12th day of October, 1795, at Guildhall, London, before

Sir JAMES SANDERSON, Bart. late Lord Mayor.

VOLUNTARY ATTESTATION.

I, JOHN BROWN, was ſeverely afflicted with an inward complaint, which affected the whole of my limbs, in which
ſtate

I continued for some time, (not being able to walk) which complaint arose from a weak, debilitated state, by a certain disorder contracted some years ago; it increased to so alarming a pitch, as to affect my head and eyes, so much as almost to deprive me of sight. By taking Dr. Brodum's Botanical Syrup and Nervous Cordial, am perfectly restored to my health, which induces me, for the benefit of my fellow creatures, to request it might be published, and fervently pray, that Dr. Brodum may continue to dispense the blessing of health to objects like me, who had long been a stranger to that great inestimable blessing.

JOHN BROWN,
Servant to S. *Slee*, at the wine vault,
No. 96, *Borough, Southwark*.

Witness—*S. Slee*, (above-mentioned) and *John Scott*, No. 3, Hat-warehouse, *Little Thames-street, Lower East Smithfield*.

To DR. BRODUM,
No. 9, Albion-street, Blackfriar's-bridge, London.

Sir,

To demonstrate the feelings of my mind, to evince the heart-felt gratitude I ought to express for my restoration to life, health, and friends, exceeds my utmost ability. To you, Sir, my dearest relatives are indebted for my existence, when every hope of recovery was lost, and dire despair sat on the countenance of every person interested in

my

my happiness. Humanity and commiseration induce me to request your publication of my situation.

Through an imprudent connection, formed when Reason had deserted its reins, I contracted a Venereal taint, and, in consequence, made application to a Surgeon, went under a regular course of mercury, with the annexed horror of frequent salivations, without eradication. The disorder was farther augmented by a cold I caught during my above situation, which deprived me of the use of my limbs. By the recommendation of a physician of eminence, I was removed to Cheltenham and Harrowgate, to try the virtues of the waters, but without relief. The hot bath was next administered with the same degree of success. In this condition I continued four years. The disorder had, notwithstanding the strictest attention, arrived to that heighth, as to produce cancerous knobs in several parts of my body, when, accidentally seeing an advertisement in the London papers, stating the situation of an old school-fellow, a Capt. George, of Hull, (who, for some years, I had not seen) I immediately wrote to him to be convinced of the fact; which, to my surprise, he informed me it was; I consulted my friends, who entertained a very indifferent opinion of advertising doctors; but my reliance on the recovery of my friend, by the same medicine, made me resolve to try its effects; I, in consequence, sent to Mr. Bristow, of Canterbury, for three bottles of Dr. Brodum's Botanical Syrup, which I took as directed. On using one bottle, I found the dreadfulness of my situation considerably augmented, and concluded the composition to be entirely mercurial, as I felt its effects

in

in a more forcible manner than even when under falivation; my friends wrote immediately to Dr. B——, who informed me, the tendency of the Syrup was of that fingular nature, as to eradicate the mercury out of the fyftem, and, of courfe, by agitating the fubtle qualities of that deftructive mineral, in its dormant receffes, it muft, in the progrefs, have the fame effect. In confequence of that information, I perfevered in it for feveral months, and, to the aftonifhment of every perfon who knew me, was reftored to that degree of health, as was almoft incredible.

A—— R——.

N. B. Since my fituation, as laft mentioned, three months have elapfed, and I am now entirely recovered; as a proof, can enter into the moft athletic exercife, without injury.

My family connections will permit the publication only of my initials, but any gentleman wifhing to be perfonally acquainted with its authenticity, may, on application to the Doctor, receive reference to my refidence.

Case of Capt. C——, of Wapping.

I Captain C——, of Wapping, was afflicted with a complaint of a venereal tendency, which materially injured my hearing, I was advifed to adopt a falivation, but the diforder had fo far entered the fyftem, as to produce holes in my legs. I was recommended fea-bathing, but without relief; but meeting with Captain Waring, of Rotherhithe, at Gibraltar, he produced me a quantity of Dr. Brodum's Botanical Syrup, which, in three months, not only eradicated the complaint, but fo far healed the fores in my leg, as to render their former appearance not perceptible, and in gratitude for my recovery, I exprefs a wifh for the publication.

Case of Mr. D——, of Theobald-road.

I was fubject to a Venereal diforder nineteen years, and during that period was under the hands of the firft men in the fcience of phyfic, who adopted every method wherein the fmalleft probability of fuccefs could be formed; and apparently, the difeafe was entirely expelled; but the alleviation was but for a moment, and then returned with redoubled force; the want of fuccefs, the affertions of entire reftoration, by thofe who undertook the cure, entirely diffipated thofe fanguine hopes I entertained of the infallibility of medical fkill. The natural confequence refulting from the inefficacy of the various methods adopted, and the violent operation of aftringent minerals, coming in contact with the difeafe, produced an ulcer on the lungs. Then the horrors of exiftence was experienced, a defcription of which would be an attempt vague and inconfiftent; thofe only who have felt that degree of mifery, can be fenfible of its effects. Without wifhing to reflect on practioners, titioners, (to whom nature has not been so liberal as their unwearied exertions merit) practical knowledge must be acknowledged far superior to theory. The contradictory assertions on the symptoms, the excruciating torture arising, had been discussed, and various motives ascribed. During this period, my dissolution was the only subject of my prayers, when I received from a friend a pamphlet of Dr. Brodum's, recommending a medicine, called the Botanical Syrup, in which was pointed out several cases of a nature strongly similar to my own; but as some person in it says he had no opinion of the merit of nostrums, I must own I entertained the same idea, but through the importunity of my friend, and being conscious I could not be in a worse situation, I sent to Dr. Brodum, and went under a regular course of his medicines, and in four months was astonishingly recovered.

[Mr. D— is entirely restored since the above statement, and has recommended the Botanical Syrup with that zeal, which he is sensible it merits.]

Though Dr. Brodum's Botanical Syrup is so well known for its efficacy, in relieving many thousands of people in certain disorders, that must inevitably have sunk into the grave, to prevent the above disorder.

As many persons, in the moment of intoxication, or from the promiscuous pursuits of pleasure, are extremely liable to endanger their health by improper connections with the *fair sex*, Dr. Brodum has the satisfaction to inform them, that he is in possession of an infallible remedy, which has never been known to fail in any instance, as a certain preventive against the venereal complaint, which will have the desired effect in twenty-four hours after connection, and which only can be had by application at the Doctor's house, (and at any hour) by asking for Dr. Brodum's *Golden Packet*, with proper directions for using it, Price 1l. 2s.

N. B. Any slight infection, the Doctor undertakes to cure in 48 hours.

Medical Facts on Venereal Complaints.

MANY perfons that have imagined themfelves to be cured of the venereal complaint, have had the misfortune to break out fix or feven years afterwards.

A proof happened in my practice the other day. A gentleman was afflicted with the fame complaint, and cured, as he thought, by the advice and prefcription of an eminent furgeon. He afterwards entered on the ftate of matrimony, four months after which he caught a violent cold in coming out of the playhoufe, that terminated in a fore throat. At this crifis I was called in, and after afking him the neceffary queftions, acquainted him that it proceeded from his old venereal complaint, but which he would not believe. He then called in the affiftance of fome apothecaries, who treated his complaint as a common fore throat, until he became fo bad, that he was compelled to apply to Dr. Vaughan, who confirmed him in the truth of what I had told him, but too late for his recovery, the venereal complaint having eaten away a part of his throat and nofe, the ravages of which could not be ftopped during his life, fo that he fell a facrifice to his obftinacy. Perfons, therefore, fhould be extremely cautious in eradicating the above complaint, than which there is nothing more beneficial than the Botanical Syrup, which is a certain remedy, without fubjecting patients to thofe dangers that attend a courfe of mercury.

CHAP. XXVI.

Observations on Sea Bathing.

THE concourse of persons who assemble at the most fashionable watering places to indulge themselves in the favourite custom of Sea Bathing, without an idea of the numerous dangers to which they are exposed, by thus immersing themselves into an element to which they are totally unaccustomed, renders it incumbent on the author of a Treatise of Health, to give them the following cautions.

When the viscera are obstructed, a spasm or cramp ensuing, occasions the dissolution of those, who, in these immersions,

merſions, for want of proper reflection, become the victims of their own temerity.

Man, undoubtedly, from his firſt formation, was taught to immerſe himſelf in cold water; the practice, therefore, muſt have immediately followed the creation of the world. To lave the body in cold water, when parched with the too oppreſſive heat of the ſun, or when over-fatigued by the common labour of the day, is certainly as great a refreſhment as it is in the power of man to experience. But before he indulges himſelf in this pleaſurable ſenſation, he ſhould acquaint himſelf with the actual ſtate of his health, leſt, by an incautious act of temerity, he ſhould bring upon himſelf a diſorder that may either occaſion him a ſpeedy or lingering diſſolution.

Cleanlinefs is fo commendable in all ages, fexes, and difpofitions, that the celebrated Lord Chefterfield has actually ranked it among the virtues, nor is there in his excellent leffons to his fon, any advice that he more ftrongly endeavours to inculcate, than a ftrict adherence to a rule, without which, neither the woman of quality, or the man of fafhion, can appear with common decency, much lefs advantage.

Animals being taught by inftinct to immerfe themfelves in cold water, for the purpofes of refrefhing themfelves after being fatigued from the intenfe heat of the fun, and wafhing off that dirt and filth that will adhere to their bodies in hot fultry weather, prefents a moft excellent example to man, who fhould regulate his feafons of bathing with extreme caution, and take efpecial care not to remain too long in the water, left
inftead

inſtead of good, evil conſequences ſhould enſue.

The voluptuary, and all perſons who, from the nature of their employments, are obliged to lead ſedentary lives, will find the cold bath moſt ſingularly ſerviceable, from its ſtrengthening the action of the ſolids, producing a free circulation, and removing crude humours, and all obſtructions that take place in the glandular ſyſtem and capillary veſſels.

Salt-water, by poſſeſſing a greater portion of gravity than any other, accelerates the motion of the blood, and through its wonderful efficacy, by ſtimulating the ſkin, promotes a free perſpiration, and prevents the patient from taking cold.

Cold bathing more eaſily prevents than removes obſtructions in the glandular

dular or lymphatic syftem, and when they have arrived at a certain pitch, thefe immerfions are often the ultimate occafion of the patient's diffolution. When the paffages of the lungs are obftructed, and any fymptoms of inflammation appear, bathing fhould carefully be avoided, as directly inimical and fraught with danger of the moft ferious and alarming nature.

Perfons of a plethoric habit, or who fubfift on grofs and high-feafoned food, run great rifque, in thefe immerfions, of breaking a blood-veffel, or producing an inflammation in the brain or vifcera, and yet none, with more avidity, or lefs thought, plunge into the fea, and although they often efcape without receiving any harm, yet the numbers whofe immediate deaths are produced by apoplexy, cramp, &c. ought to be a fufficient warning to deter others from fanctioning fo dangerous a practice.

Bathing

Bathing should never be adopted until the body has been prepared by some active alterative medicine.

The bracing qualities of cold bathing are not conducive of greater benefit to any description of patients, than those who have experienced a derangement in the nervous syftem; yet they ought to use it with extreme moderation and care, left through the natural weakness of the bowels in those situations, the viscera should become obstructed, and the patient not able to bear the cold which is the continual attendant upon this element. The best and surest mode of regulating the practice of Bathing is, to begin about the middle of the day, when the heat is most intense, by which means the body will not suffer, in the first instance, but will become so prepared by habit, that that severity of the morning, or of weather, which would otherwise

occasion

occasion the moſt fatal effects, may be enjoyed with ſafety, and produce a pleaſure abſolutely inexpreſſible.

Danger is always to be apprehended, and often found by ſudden tranſitions from heat to cold.

Were parents to accuſtom their children to the uſe of the cold bath from their earlieſt infancy, its tonic powers would prevent the ſcrofula, rickets, and many other diſorders, from which there is otherwiſe no preventive, and, at the ſame time, improve their ſtrength, facilitate their growth, and, by removing thoſe ſickly, languid, and emaciated aſpects, which are the concomitants of illneſs, their countenances would exhibit thoſe inſignia of health, which are real bleſſings to all who inherit ſo invaluable a poſſeſſion.

The generality of diseases incident to childhood, would be obviously prevented by this excellent custom being adopted, under proper restrictions, from the birth.

Young men should systematically avoid too frequent bathing, which, as well as the rash practice of continuing too long in the water at a time, has, in innumerable instances, brought them to an early and untimely grave.

When the constitution is debilitated and relaxed, weaknesses occur in the back and reins, relaxations and swellings appear in the joints, symptoms of scrofula, nervous affections, &c. the cold bath, by invigorating the muscular system, produces the best of effects, especially when the state of the body has been prepared by so sanative a medicine as the Nervous Cordial.

The time of the day most congenial for bathing is, undoubtedly, in the morning, or before the stomach has taken any portion of animal food, and the mode of immersion should be by descending into this nutritive element with the greatest possible velocity, and, by wetting the head first, the blood and humours are effectually prevented from being propelled towards that part, as is otherwise inevitably the case. A perseverance in this rule will effectually prevent violent head-achs, &c. which would certainly originate from the adoption of any other mode.

The cold bath, by being continued in too long, prevents the excellent intention for which it was designed, relaxes the nerves, cramps the muscles, chills the blood, and occasions an excessive flux of humours to be propelled towards the head.

This very circumstance has frequently compleated the destruction of several of our most expert swimmers, who, by being too partial to an exercise in which they have become such proficients, have fallen victims to their pleasure, or rather folly, before any assistance could be procured.

A single and instantaneous immersion of the whole body in the cold bath, answers a much more salutary purpose than if the bathers continue in it for a longer period, after which, the person should be carefully dried, and adopt, for some hours afterwards, healthy and wholesome exercise.

An excellent preparatory for every person to observe before he adventures on a course of Sea Bathing, is to take especial care that all the nerves, arteries, veins, and vessels, are open, and entirely free from the least obstruction.

The

The action of the water has so astonishing an effect upon the system of circulation, that the blood, and all the animal juices, are propelled with the greatest rapidity through every fibre of the frame, and when they are suddenly impeded in their progress, by an obstruction, the immediate consequences are, the bursting of a vein, or a spasm occurring on a vital part, than which nothing is more certain of producing immediate death.

Experience has convinced the author of this Treatise, that nothing can so safely and completely prepare all persons who are induced to undergo a course of bathing, as a strict adherence in taking about two spoonfuls of the Nervous Cordial, regularly about an hour before each immersion. A month's preparation with gentle physic should likewise be strictly observed.

This will remove all obstructions in the vessels, clean and strengthen the viscera and vital organs, gently open and lubricate the bowels, and prepare the body to derive those advantages which were obviously the primary causes of Sea Bathing becoming so general in this country.

That description of persons who are induced to bathe from being subject to eruptions arising from vitiated humours, scurvy, &c. will experience particular relief in taking the Botanical Syrup one hour before bathing, and immediately afterwards, to the quantity of two table spoonfuls, which may be encreased by regular gradations to four.

While discussing the advantages resulting from bathing at large, those which peculiarly depend on the use of the warm bath must not be neglected,

and

and here it muſt be obvious, that in alṁoſt every inſtance in which the cold bath would threaten miſchief, the warm bath muſt produce conſiderable benefit. To thoſe whoſe maſculine fibres are relaxed, either conſtitutionally, or from the influence of ſome late diſeaſe, the ſtudious, the ſedentary, and the ſcorbutic, the warm bath muſt be deleterious ; while the rheumatic, the aſthmatic, the gouty, and thoſe afflicted with ſudden ſpaſms, inflammations in the viſcera, or internal obſtructions of any kind, will be ſure to derive a conſiderable mitigation, and, in many caſes, a complete cure for the unhappy ſymptoms under which they labour.

This diſtinction and diſcrimination between the advantages of the hot and cold bath ſhould be, therefore, minutely attended to, as of infinite conſequence to the benefit of the patient who is about to to bathe; and it is from want of such attention that bathing has frequently been condemned, when, on the contrary, it ought to have been extolled, and the ignorance or inattention of the patient, or his friends, to have been condemned in its ftead.

Dr. Brodum finally requests to conclude with the following Address.

BOLD claims to extraordinary cures are so often the effects of imposition or of arrogance, that the regular bred physician always feels some awkwardness in recommending to public notice any uncommon discovery he may have made during the exercise of his profession. Motives of false delicacy, however, should not engage him to suppress what may be of the utmost advantage to society, when confirmed by repeated experiments.

Dr. Brodum is induced by so just a consideration, thus to proclaim to the world, the result of his long and extensive five private practice. His character and situation in life place him beyond the reach of envious and illiberal attacks. He is enabled to despise any silly insinuation of his dealing in nostrums; such a bubble, raised by envy or malignity, must burst at the slightest touch of common sense. Are not the recipes of the most celebrated physicians their nostrums or specifics? Do they not prescribe from a presumption that such medicines will take effect? And, surely, the more proofs we can give of the efficacy of a medicine, the stronger claims we have to rational confidence. That confidence must also be increased, when the physician makes up the medicine himself, and thus guards the patient from the danger of trusting prescriptions to the ignorance, incapacity, and carelessness of some of the apothecaries' apprentices.

The

The Doctor flatters himſelf, his ſucceſs in reſtoring many thouſands in the three kingdoms, who had laboured under the moſt dreadful, and hitherto incurable diſorders, ſeveral years, will render him more eſſential ſervice than mere pompoſity of words. He is ſenſible how unuſual it is for the faculty in England to circulate accounts of cures through the medium of pamphlets, bills, &c. But are the lives of our fellow-creatures to be ſacrificed to ſilly prejudice? Is the form laid down by any particular ſet of men to be preferred to the dictates of humanity and common ſenſe? Or can the ſuggeſtions of malignity and envy have more weight with the world than the full evidence of thoſe whom the Doctor has relieved from ſickneſs and deſpair? Their grateful and well-meant teſtimonies, and, in particular, the very diſtinguiſhed ſignatures of ſeveral of the lords and ladies

ladies attendant on their majefties will, he doubts not, carry fome degree of weight with the impartial.

Prior to clofing this addrefs, the Doctor, with permiffion, begs leave to propofe one queftion to his criticifing friends---" Why are not cures publifhed in a newfpaper, equally worthy the notice of Valetudinarians, as thofe performed with greater privacy?" If any man is in poffeffion of a valuable remedy, is he not a far more worthy and beneficial member of the community than thofe, who, from motives beft known to themfelves, withhold their falutary virtues from the public? In early times, the perfons who had any fuccefs in curing diforders, defcribed the progrefs of their medicines on the walls of the temples; if formerly that method was received with that gratitude the arduous tafk merited, why
fhould

should cures advertised, be looked on with contempt? The Doctor will therefore challenge with confidence, secure in the integrity of his motives, and yielding to the force of this just observation, that " to with-hold a remedy from the afflicted, is, in fact, little less than murder!"

Physic is now become a *complicated Science*, and ought, undoubtedly, to be practised only by men of long and successful *Experience* in *Anatomy*, *Surgery*, and *Chemistry*: And the Afflicted, who purchase medicines, ought to be well convinced that they apply to an *ingenious Physician, one who is regularly admitted to practice*, and not to an artful and self-recommended impostor.

But were the public to demand of such men their right to the noble Art of of PHYSIC, their iniquitous proceedings would foon be put a ftop to; and that the public may be guarded againft the forgeries of thofe empyrics, Dr. Brodum here fubjoins the Diploma, or Certificate of his Medical Degree.

THE DIPLOMA,
OR TESTIMONIAL OF THE
DEGREE of DOCTOR in PHYSIC,
GRANTED TO
WILLIAM BRODUM,
At the MARISCHAL COLLEGE and UNIVERSITY of ABERDEEN.

(Tranſlated from the Latin Copy) viz.
To all and ſingular the Perſons who may read, peruſe, and to whoſe knowledge this Privilege of the Degree of Doctor in Phyſic, by Us granted, may come—We, Alexander Donaldſon, Doctor of Phyſic, in the Mariſchal College and Univerſity of Aberdeen, wiſh Health!

AS it has been an ancient and laudable Cuſtom, that thoſe who have applied themſelves to Learning, with much labour and aſſiduous Study, ſhould be honoured with ſome ſingular Mark of Diſtinction, as a Teſtimony of their ſucceſsful Perſeverance, and a Reward for their extraordinary Merit, that the rising Generation may be incited by such Examples to pursue the like arduous, but glorious Career of Erudition and Virtue:

Therefore, We, Alexander Donaldson, with the unanimous consent of the Rector, Principal, and the other Professors of the said University, do create, declare, and appoint the above WILLIAM BRODUM, *Doctor of Physic*, with full Licence and Authority to exercise his profession, delivering Lectures, teaching and explaining the Art of Physic, as well as to exercise his Profession in every part of the World; and we also confer upon him, by Virtue of this public Instrument, all the Privileges, Immunities, and Honours annexed to that degree, in their utmost Extent, according to the Form, Spirit, and Intention of the Statutes of this College and University.

In Proof and Attestation of which, we have signed the Great Seal of our University, with our respective Names and Signatures to this Diploma.

ALEXANDER DONALDSON,
    Doctor and Professor of Physic.
GEORGIUS CAMPBELL, *Gymna-siarch*, S. S. T. P.
J. BEATTIE, L.L.D.M. or P.P.
JO. STUART, Lit. Gr. P.
RO. HAMILTON, L.L.D.P.P.
JA. BEATTIE, Jun. P.P.

SIGILLUM
Collegii Marischal
Aberdonen.

In confequence of the great repute of the medicine, it has induced a number of Quacks to counterfeit and vend them as genuine, who ride about the country and deliver bills in my name, who fend their fervants to call for Dr. Brodum's books, and offer their own papers inftead; therefore the public will remark that the Doctor never fends for any of his pamphlets again.---As there is a perfon who calls himfelf a Doctor, entitles himfelf a Phyfician, imitates my writings, and advertifes a medicine and a publication in name fimilar to mine, and alfo copies my advertifements verbatim from the different newfpapers, feveral

several of which have been refused insertion by the printers, as being an exact copy of what they had previously inserted for me. Against this insidious mode of Conduct the Doctor requests the public to guard themselves, and assures them (particularly those who may doubt the truth of this) that he is in possession of a letter, written by his own father, which will pretty clearly prove, that he does not possess all the *wisdom* of a SOLOMON! The unguarded public are desired to pay attention to the following :---that on the seal of my medicines is the name of Dr. BRODUM, and in each direction bill is my Degree, authenticated by the College of Physicians, as a regular bred man; and observe, it is marked with F. R. H. S.——
And if the public do not find my Arms and Degree (as before-mentioned) on the bottles, they may be assured they are not genuine.

Observe,

Obferve, the Doctor does not travel the country again, as he has entirely re-eftablifhed his health, and in confequence of his prefence being continually neceffary at his houfe in London, where he gives advice.---No other perfon of the name of Brodum is in England.

The unprecedented fuccefs of this publication has caufed a literary theft or piracy to be impofed on the public, in the expectation that they would honour it with a fimilar welcome reception, to that which diftinguifhed the "Guide to Old Age," but it no more refembles his work than the mediocrity of the talents of *Saul*, did the inexpreffible wifdom of SOLOMON! The public have in this inftance efcaped the fnare that was laid for their incredulity. Many copies of this work being attempted to be foifted upon individuals---Perfons are requefted to to be cautious in enquiring for Dr. Brodum's "Guide to Old Age," since there are Guides to many other things, but to none that are more serviceable to the generality of mankind.

N. B. The Syrup is in tin bottles; the Nervous Cordial in flint bottles, with the Doctor's arms, as under, i. e. three dolphins---crest, a bear.

Whoever will apprehend any person or persons of the above description, shall receive a reward of TEN GUINEAS,

on

on conviction of the offender or offenders, by applying to Dr. Brodum.

It will be neceſſary the Doctor ſhould ſee ſuch patients as are afflicted with deafneſs or loſs of ſight.

EXTERNAL

EXTERNAL APPEARANCE

NECESSARY

IN LIFE.

LORD Chesterfield particularly advises cleanliness, not only as necessary to health, but the success of our fortunes in life, but with so slothful a complaint as any disease that has the least analogy to the Scrofula, indolence will naturally prevent either of the sexes from profiting by this excellent observation.

Erup-

Eruptions in the Face.

The inconsistent doctrine of those who recommend external applications, for internal complaints, is obviated in the following simple question; will the fur which adheres to the inside of a kettle, or boiler, be removed by washing the outside? The same comparison may be made respecting the human frame. Can an internal complaint be removed by an external application? These questions are left to be answered by every reader, which will shew the ridiculousness of inculcating this doctrine while the infallibility of

Dr. Brodum's Botanical Syrup,

is evinced in the extraordinary cures that daily appear in the papers; particularly in cases of the above nature; Dr. Brodum, as a regular Physician, has been known many years, and not as a Nostrum

Nostrum Vender. His motive for publishing this advertisement, is to secure the health of the public from the danger that attends external application, which, to his knowledge, has proved fatal to many who have placed in it an improper confidence.

Social Happiness.

Marriage should be the foundation of Social Happiness, which is often disturbed through the parties that form the union not taking those precautions which would secure them the enjoyment of that great domestic blessing. Thus would those who are afflicted with an internal or external scorbutic habit of body, by taking that admirable purifier of the blood,

Dr. Brodum's Botanical Syrup,

secure the health of their future offspring, and thus, inftead of meriting the leaft reproach, have the fatisfaction to deferve the higheft encomium. Thofe to whom the health of their family are dear, will doubtlefs acknowledge the truth of this trite obfervation.

Be pleafed to afk for Dr. Brodum's Botanical Syrup, becaufe there are various forts of Syrup, advertifed in tin bottles, they go by the name of Vegetable Syrup, the Syrup, &c.

Directions for taking the Nervous Cordial.

Of this ftrengthening medicine, take two tea-fpoonfuls four times a day, for fix weeks, in half a glafs of Port-wine, or cold water, fweetened, if you choofe it; but if the difeafe be defperate, then indeed

indeed it fhould be taken in a quarter of a pint of wild valerian tea, in the morning fafting, about eleven o'clock, at four in the afternoon, and an hour before you go to bed. If obftinate, add to every dofe of the drops, in the fame glafs of Port-wine, water, &c. one table-fpoonful of HUXHAM's TINCTURE of BARK, which may be had in pint or half-pint bottles, at any chemift's fhop.

Bilious Complaints.

Should the patient be afflicted with this diforder, he muft begin with two tea-fpoonfuls the firft week, four the fecond, and fix the third; take every fortnight an emetic, and work it off with camomile tea.

Difeafes of the Head.

The medicine is to be taken as in nervous diforders.---In fits as directed.

―――

Difeafes which in general are natural to Women.

Such ladies whofe ages are young, and bordering on the ftate of womanhood, muft take of the medicine three tea-fpoonfuls twice a day, in a glafs of Port-wine, and bathe the legs in warm water every night, for three weeks---a handful of falt to be put into the water, and to mix half an ounce of rhubarb, with half an ounce of prepared fteel, then divide the fame into twelve powders, and take one every third night.

To such Ladies as are in the Decline of Nature.

To take of the above medicine three tea-spoonfuls, three times a day, in a glass of Madeira wine; and to take half an ounce of tincture of rhubarb, half an ounce of tincture of senna, half an ounce of stomach tincture, and half an ounce of syrup of buckthorn, mixed together, one-half to be taken once a month, as physic.

———

To those who labour under a Consumption and Asthma.

To take two tea-spoonfuls of the medicine, three times a day, in white wine, to boil six onions in a pint of vinegar, to sweeten it with honey, and to take one table spoonful every three hours.

Dropsy, Palsy, and Rheumatism.

To take four tea-spoonfuls twice a day, in a glass of Port-wine, and dissolve one ounce of camphor in a cup of sweet oil, to bathe the parts affected.

Serious Exhortation to those who have been addicted to a certain Practice common to either Sex, which often is the Occasion of many dreadful Disorders.

The above medicine is particularly recommended, which strengthens the weakened parts---to take three tea-spoonfuls every three hours, and to make a decoction of four ounces of bark, two ounces of comfrey-root, boil it it in a quart of red wine, and reduce it to a pint; to take two table-spoonfuls with three tea-spoonfuls of the Nervous Cordial, every three hours.

REGIMEN.

Avoid salted and dried meats, pork, geese, fish, cheese, much butter, rich sauces, acids, Indian tea, coffee, cyder, raw fruit, and all flatulent vegetables; you may eat at meals horse-raddish, mustard, celery, asparagus, water-cresses, and all the warmer sallads; roasted meats and poultry are preferable to boiled, as they afford more nutrition in quantity; all fried and broiled meats should be avoided, as they turn rancid on the stomach: breakfast on cocoa, rosemary tea, or get some genseng and cut it up, and make three drachms into a pint of tea. Eat light suppers of easy digestion, sago, panado,

panado, water gruel, with a glafs of wine and nutmeg, new laid eggs poached, oyfters, roafted apples, or fomething elfe not oppreffive, nor reluctant to digeftion. Avoid an indolent fedentary life, and ufe exercife freely, and change of air, adopting fome kind of labour, not too fatiguing.

As it is neceffary the body fhould be kept moderately open, it may be effected by taking thirty grains of rhubarb, or drinking fenna tea occafionally.

The genfeng can be had at any Druggift's Shop.

Direc-

Directions for taking this Syrup in Scrofula, Scurvy, Scorbutic Eruptions, and in all morbid Affections of the Human Body.

MALES should begin this Syrup in the quantity of two table-spoonfuls, one hour after breakfast, and the same quantity at night, going to rest; gradually increasing the dose to four table-spoonfuls each time.

FEMALES may begin in the quantity of one table-spoonful, morning and night, and gradually increasing to three each time.

CHIL-

CHILDREN, from two to five years old, may begin in the quantity of three tea-spoonfuls, night and morning, gradually increasing the dose to six each time. Children from six to twelve years old, may begin in the quantity of four tea-spoonfuls, night and morning, gradually increasing the dose to eight each time.

———

YOUTH of either sex, from thirteen years and upwards, may begin in the quantity of one table-spoonful, gradually increasing the dose to three each time. The medicine is always to be taken in some light simple vehicle, as tea of any kind, milk and water, or such like. No particular regimen is necessary, but temperance in all things will be found most conducive to convalescence.

For cancers, evils, or sores, take an ounce of white lead, and an ounce of olive oil; simmer it into a salve, and apply it to the part affected---every morning a plaster; washing the wound with a little water gruel.

To those ladies and gentlemen bordering on the state of matrimony, the Doctor would particularly recommend the Botanical Syrup, (prior to their appearance before the Altar of Hymen) who are in the smallest degree apprehensive of the system not being entirely sound, or subject to relaxations of the solids.

Persons who do not know the cause from whence their complaints originate, the doctor, to relieve anxiety, informs those thofe who wifh to receive benefit without a conference, that on their fending a guinea, with their morning urine, and defcribing the particulars of their cafe, they may derive equally the fame benefit; his fcientific knowledge of various diforders, by means of urine, having eftablifhed his fame. Thofe not wifhing to receive medicines of his agents, may receive them from his houfe in London, by addreffing a line, poft-paid.

Any lady or gentleman who is exceedingly ill, had better make a perfonal application to Dr. Brodum, that he may have it in his power to give prefcriptions, or other advice; if it fhould be found neceffary, that their diforder may be removed with all convenient fpeed; or any lady or gentleman whofe cafe will not permit them to quit their own houfes, may be waited upon with the greateft attention, by the Doctor, at five guineas per week.

Per-

Perfons who apply for thefe medicines, will pleafe to take notice, that it will be in vain to expect any relief from this remedy, without punctuality; for taking a bottle or two properly, then leaving off for fome days and beginning again, will be of no kind of fervice. It muft be taken regular; and in fome cafes it hath required the quantity neceffary for a perfect cure to be taken before the patient has perceived that he hath obtained any relief; therefore, perfons in the country, who wifh to go through a regular courfe of it, fhould take care to have a proper fupply of Doctor Brodum's Reftorative Nervous Cordial.

Any gentleman or lady who may have any internal or external complaint, that may require the particular and conftant attendance of the Doctor, may be accommodated with elegant apartments, fit for the reception of any gentleman or lady in the kingdom, with proper attendance, and the use of a carriage, (if required) on terms that will meet with approbation.

It will be necessary the Doctor should see such patients as are afflicted with deafness or loss of sight; or send their cases by letters or parcel, to the Doctor, (post or carriage paid) with his usual fee.

Personal consultations at the Doctor's house, every Monday, Tuesday, and Wednesday.

The Botanical Syrup and Restorative Nervous Cordial to be had at the Doctor's House, No. 9, Albion-street, in bottles at 1l. 2s.—11s. 6d.—and 5s. 5d. each, (duty included; at Jeboult and Co.'s (late Bacon) Oxford-street; Pidding's Medicine Warehouse, No. 76, Oxford-street, near

near the Pantheon; Ward's Medicinal Warehouse, No. 324, Holborn, opposite Gray's Inn; Williams's, Perfumer to his Majesty, No. 41, Pall Mall; E. Newberry's, corner of St. Paul's Church-yard; Mr. Tutt's, and Mr. Bolton, Royal Exchange; Bourgeois and Co. No. 32, Hay-market.

Also of the following Agents:

Blake, Maidstone
Bristow, Canterbury
Baxter, Perfumer, Edinburgh
Baker, Southampton
Brown, Tolsey, Bristol
Burkitt, Sudbury
Blakeney, Windsor
Binns, Leeds
Bacon, Norwich
Crutwell, Bath
Crutwell, Sherborne
Collins, Salisbury
Clackar, Printer, Chelmsford
Chalmers and Co. Aberdeen
Cox, Hair-dresser, Tunbridge
Coveney, Feversham
Donaldson, Portsmouth
Dicey, Northampton
Downes, Yarmouth

Ethrington, Chatham
Trueman, Exeter
Tesseyman, York
Walker, Hereford
Stainbank, Boston
Albin, Newport, in the Isle of Wight
Gee, Cambridge
Drummond, Lincoln
Meggit, Wakefield
Simmonds, Blandford
Merritt and Wright, Printers, Liverpool
Town, Gainsboro'
Marshall, Lynn
Barnikel, Plymouth
Hodges, Sherborne
Wood, Shrewsbury
Lynch, Druggist, Market-street, Manchester
Binns, Halifax
Fletcher, Chester
Walker, Hereford

Mrs.

[184]

Mrs. Sanderson, Doncaster
Billings, Liverpool
Wheeler, Manchester
Coudroy and Boden, ditto
Pytt, Gloucester
Raikes, ditto
Gregory, Leicester
Payne, Saffron Walden
Quarnborough, Grantham
Mrs. Silver, Chemist, Margate
Swinney, Birmingham
Smart, Reading
Symond, Canterbury
Goadby, Sherborne
M'Donald, Glasgow
Mrs. Clifton, Stationer, Durham
Kelly, North Shields
Messrs. Ridge, Newark
Jacob, Peterborough
White, Wisbeach
Wood, Weymouth
Fisher, Bookseller, Penzance
Mennont, Printer, Glasgow
Fuller, Newbury
Watts, Mercury Office, Oxford
Miss Jones, ditto
Graham, Sunderland
Gill, ditto
Walker, Printer, Newcastle.

And to be had of all the Booksellers and Printers in the principal market towns of the three kingdoms.

As a further proof of the great demand for these medicines, Messrs. Goldthwaite and Baldwin are appointed wholesale venders at Philadelphia, in America.

☞ The bottles at 1l. 2s. contain five of 5s. 5d.

ADDITIONAL

ADDITIONAL CASES.

Another remarkable Proof of the great Efficacy of Doctor Brodum's Botanical Syrup.

A Gentleman, residing in Portland Place, had been a long time tormented with a humour in his blood, which caused eruptions in various parts of the body, accompanied with a dry, scaly appearance of the skin, burning heat, and perpetual itching, almost insufferable. Being a gentleman of considerable fortune, he was exceedingly anxious to get well; and for that purpose, consulted many eminent Gentlemen of the Faculty successively, but to no purpose, for the disorder, instead of declining, increased. Having frequently read advertisements respecting Dr. Brodum's Botanical Syrup, he called at Mr. Pidding's Medicine Warehouse, opposite the Pantheon, Oxford-street, to make inquiries respecting it; and being perfectly satisfied with the references Mr. Pidding gave him to different persons who had found benefit from it in a similar situation, and who had purchased the Medicine at his Warehouse, he made trial of a bottle, which operated in such a desirable manner, that he was induced to persevere, and after continuing the use of it for about a month, he was perfectly cured.

N. B. As this Case is so very respectable, and at the same time so interesting to those who are troubled with scrofulus or scorbutic complaints, any person may be informed of further particulars, by applying to Mr. Pidding, No. 76, Oxford-street, opposite the Pantheon, who is one of Dr. Brodum's Agents for the Sale of his Medicines.

The Letter which inclosed the under-mentioned extraordinary Cure, was tranſmitted by J. GREGORY, Brighthelmſtone Library, Sept. 26, 1796.

Mrs. Allen, of North-ſtreet, Brighton, was afflicted with a violent Nervous complaint, and had the advice of the moſt eminent of the Faculty, who recommended her to Briſtol Hotwells, where ſhe found no relief; but by applying to Dr. Brodum, and taking his Nervous Cordial, is now quite recovered, and enjoys better health than ſhe has done for ſome years.

To Dr. BRODUM, London.

SIR,

The increaſing reputation of your Nervous Cordial and Botanical Syrup, has of late been aſtoniſhing in this populous part of the kingdom. You will have the goodneſs to ſend us another freſh ſupply—the demand for the laſt has been urgent in the extreme; and its efficacy is ſuch here, as to ſecure its permanent reputation.

Your obedient ſervants,

COWDROY and BODEN.

St. Mary's-gate, Mancheſter,
  Nov. 1, 1796.

To Dr. BRODUM.

Exeter, Nov. 12, 1796.

Confidering the variety of cafes publifhed in various Prints, proving the efficacious virtues of your medicines, it may be efteemed unneceffary for us to fay any thing in their favour; but from the pureft motives we are induced to affert, that in the courfe of all our trade, no medicine has ever gained equal refpect, and had fo rapid a fale, as your Botanical Syrup and Nervous Cordial, which is corroborated by the numerous cures performed by it in Exeter and its environs.

TREWMAN and SON.

To Dr. BRODUM.

SIR,

I return you my fincere thanks for the cure that was received by your excellent medicines. My fon, John Southwell, was afflicted with a bilious complaint, which brought on a violent pain, and vomiting, proceeding from a bad digeftion of the ftomach, from the collection of bile. In this deplorable fituation he was four months; but by taking two bottles of your Nervous Cordial, was perfectly cured, as witnefs our hands,

JOHN and ANN SOUTHWELL,

The parents have declared unto us the
the above is true,
William Belgrave, Wm. Treen, Bankers, *Uppingham.*
Thomas Hill, Woolftapler, *Rutlandfhire.*

Many

Many difpute about Deafnefs being incurable, but Dr. Brodum's method has never yet failed.

SAMUEL TEBBUT, of Oundle, was deaf, and had a pain in his head, which proceeded from a nervous complaint, for four years; but by applying to and taking Dr. Brodum's Nervous Cordial, was perfectly cured.

———

Captain Brooks cured of a deep decline.

Lady M'Lean, Fitzroy-fquare, cured of a nervous complaint.

Major Wallen, cured of deafnefs.

Mifs Debaw, Finfbury-fquare, cured of a cancer.

The particular cafes of the numbers cured would be too tedious to mention:

Thirty cured of a Decline—Ten of a Dropfy—Twenty of Deafnefs—Seven reftored to their Sight—Hundreds of the Scurvy, Evil, Eruptions in the Face, Sore Legs, and certain Diforders.

ADVICE

ADVICE

TO

BATHERS AT BATH HOT WELLS, SEA BATHERS, &c. &c.

DR. Brodum begs leave to recommend the BOTANICAL SYRUP (the virtues of which are acknowledged by persons of the first fashion and distinction) to Bathers immediately after quitting the Bath, and one hour before, and in particular to those who are subject to eruptions arising from vitiated humours, scurvy, &c. The quantity to be taken each time, two table-spoonfuls.

To nervous and debilitated constitutions in general, owing to an irregular course of life, as hard drinking, excesfive grief, and thofe debilities brought on by not knowing the dangerous tendency of a certain habit contracted at an early age, the Doctor recommends the Nervous Cordial, two tea-fpoonfuls of which to be taken an hour before bathing, and one after. Ten minutes walk after is neceffary.

The Nervous Cordial has been particularly efficacious in America, where feveral thoufand perfons have been faved during the late alarming prevalence of the yellow fever. The Doctor particularly recommends the above medicine to perfons going out to the Eaft or Weft Indies, where the change of air and climate require the aid of medicine, to prevent the dangerous confequence which muft refult in various conftitutions.

The

The five-guinea bottles, which contain equal to six guinea bottles, are *only* to be had at the Doctor's house.

A number of cures performed at Margate, Southampton, Bath, Briftol, Harrowgate, Dover, &c. &c. in the courfe of the laft feafon, on feveral ladies and gentlemen, who, from their elevated fituation in life, will not permit their names being publifhed.

The Doctor begs leave to teftify his thanks for the multiplicity of cures he has received, and to prevent any erroneous idea being formed of his wifh to publifh fuch ftatements as are not confiftent with the fituation of the parties, to obviate every unpleafant idea, perfons addreffing, may only place their initials, and an anfwer will be returned. A. B. To be left at   No.   Street or Town where they refide.

reside. The afflicted may rest assured, that they will receive proper advice, with every thing necessary to restore them to their former health and vigour.

www.ingramcontent.com/pod-product-compliance
Lightning Source LLC
Chambersburg PA
CBHW032144160426
43197CB00008B/768